An A–Z of Parenting for Faith

BRF Ministries

15 The Chambers, Vineyard
Abingdon OX14 3FE
+44 (0)1865 319700 | brf.org.uk

Bible Reading Fellowship (BRF) is a charity (233280)
and company limited by guarantee (301324),
registered in England and Wales

EU Authorised Representative: Easy Access System Europe –
Mustamäe tee 50, 10621 Tallinn, Estonia, **gpsr.requests@easproject.com**

ISBN 978 1 80039 399 8
First published 2025
All rights reserved

FEATURING WISDOM FROM
RACHEL TURNER AND FRIENDS

AN A–Z OF
PARENTING FOR FAITH
BITESIZE WISDOM FROM THE PODCAST
EDITED BY LUCY RYCROFT,
BECKY SEDGWICK AND ANNA HAWKEN

BRF
Ministries

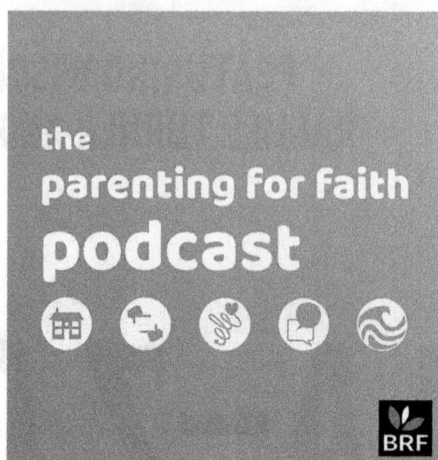

Listen to the Parenting for Faith podcast!

The Parenting for Faith podcast is here to equip you, wherever you are, whatever you're doing, to help the children and teens in your life to meet and know God. A new episode is released every Tuesday in term time.

parentingforfaith.org/podcast

CONTENTS

INTRODUCTION

Welcome to this A–Z of podcast wisdom from Parenting for Faith.

Parenting your kids for faith is full of adventure! Along the way, your kids will grow and change, you'll grow and change, and you'll encounter new seasons and new situations – good and bad. And you get to disciple your kids through it all.

One of the things we often say at Parenting for Faith is that there's no one way to help children – of any age – meet and know God. Every family, every child is unique, and you get to disciple your children in the ways that work for you and for them. God has placed us in communities of faith to support and encourage us as we do that. The Parenting for Faith podcast is one of those communities: a gang of people on the same journey of helping the kids in their lives meet and know God. Our guests' stories and experiences provide a rich seam of advice for you to mine – great nuggets of wisdom from the first five years of the Parenting for Faith podcast.

We've deliberately not covered 'situational' topics, such as additional needs or adoption and fostering, as they are too broad for us to do justice to in this format. Instead, we've covered topics that many parents and carers are likely to encounter at one stage or other. Each chapter contains questions to help you apply what you've read to your own unique situation, whether that's as a foster parent, a single parent, a parent or carer of multiple siblings... you get the gist.

No chapter will give you the final word on any topic! There's so much we could say, but we've stuck to our goal of condensing each one to a short, bitesize chapter that you can pick up and read in just a few minutes. There are 52 chapters, so you could pick one a week for a whole year, or you might want to just dip in and flick to the chapter that catches your eye.

Either way, if you like what you read, why not listen to the relevant podcast episode (you can listen for free online at **parentingforfaith.org/podcast**)?

We've added in the episode number next to the contributor's name: the 'S' tells you which season and the 'E' which episode; for example, S5E2 refers to Season 5, Episode 2.

The views expressed in this book belong to the contributors and don't necessarily reflect the views of all the other co-contributors. And, to repeat, none of this is the final word on any topic. You can talk to other parents or people, check out other podcasts or books, or speak to wise people at church. But in case it's helpful, where relevant we've put links you might want to follow up at the end of each chapter and some ideas for next steps.

At Parenting for Faith, we have some core ideas that we talk about, so you'll find our guests talking about those ideas too. If these are new to you, you will find an appendix on page 217 which covers our five Key Tools and core concepts and highlights more of what we offer.

Our prayer is that this book equips and encourages you as you go on this wonderful and sometimes extraordinary adventure of parenting the kids God has given you.

The Parenting for Faith team

parenting for **faith**®

parentingforfaith.org

A

ADVENT

RACHEL TURNER, SUSIE YEATES AND LUCY RYCROFT

The big picture

RACHEL S1E11

However you choose to do Advent – whether you go big or small – I would encourage you to explore with your child how they can express their hearts to God. Out of their expression to God of what's on their minds, they can begin to ask him for the things that are on their heart for themselves and other people, as Jesus comes into our families.

Praying through Advent

SUSIE S1E11

Every day during December, each of our children has a star sticker. On it, they write the name of somebody they know or love, and they pray for them that they'll meet with Jesus in a certain situation, that the Holy Spirit will come. It might be someone who's sick or someone who otherwise needs to know Jesus is with them. They know that the season of Jesus coming is actually Jesus coming for their friends and for their family as well for them.

Sometimes people had real problems, but we didn't know about it. The children would write the name of that person and we would text them to say the kids had prayed for them that day. They'd say, 'That's amazing, because I'm going through a hard time at work, and it's really good to know that God is with me in it.' God knew that and prompted our children, even before that person had managed to communicate with us.

Redeeming Advent

LUCY S1E50

I find it so hard to focus on Jesus in the run-up to Christmas – I'm probably not alone in this! You've got loads to do anyway, then on top of that you've got all this additional stuff in December, and then once kids are in school you've got this whole new level of Christmas craziness – it's just this huge whirlwind of activity and stuff to do. As Christians, we try retain a focus on Jesus, but it's just so difficult to do because these things threaten to take over.

It's not about scrapping every single fun thing to do at Christmas; it's about taking these aspects of Christmas and using them to glorify God. My tip would be to 'put the blinkers on': have a focus, know what you're doing and who you're celebrating. I'm not saying don't go and see Santa or go to the pantomime, but have an aim of what you're trying to get to, on or around 25 December, because there's a huge amount of rubbish that goes on during December.

Even as adults it's very difficult to focus on Jesus at Christmas – but for children, especially young children who tend to see things in black and white, it's even harder not to be confused by all the stuff going on. Kids need help in establishing what's important. I always said – from when our kids were tiny – that I never wanted them confused about what we were celebrating at Christmas. Repeating that mantra to myself every Advent helps me because then I don't feel stressed about what we haven't done or what we haven't seen, because I know that's not really for our family.

Follow-up

- 'Christmas' (p. 40) and 'Santa' (p. 168) chapters
- Lucy Rycroft, *Redeeming Advent* (Gilead, 2019)
- **thehopefilledfamily.com** (Lucy Rycroft)

Next steps

- What do you want to focus on this Advent?
- How could you help your family have an outward focus during Advent?
- What might your child need to help them express their heart to God?

A

ARGUMENTS

RACHEL TURNER S7E14

To me, an argument is a red flag that says we need a conversation; it's two people with competing values, trying to express themselves and be understood, getting emotional in the moment. Our job, as parents, is to try to understand our kids.

I'm not 100% sure we want our children to always do what we ask. Our goal is to stretch, grow and help these kids form their own internal sense of who they are, what is right and wrong, and how to love God.

More than obedience

This is more than just how we convince our kids to do what we want. It's about how we parent our kids to be who they're called to be when they hit a conflict with us.

For example, you're trying to get out of the house to go to school. You're just looking for obedience, but they're resisting. Either then or later, ask what is going on underneath the behaviour. Kids don't always have the language to communicate what they're feeling. You could ask:

- How does it feel when I ask you to do something quickly?
- What is our ideal getting-out-of-the-house scenario for you?
- What does getting out of the house peacefully look like for you?

Secondly, explain things. So often we communicate for obedience rather than understanding. If our goal is for children to manage themselves, we need to share the values behind what we're asking them to do. Then we're on the same team and can find a solution. It could be that we need to start getting ready earlier, set a timer or use a tick list.

Talking about sin

As adults, when we are aware we have sinned, we come to God knowing he loves and understands us. We then apologise out of that connection with him. That's a good model for us: first to make sure our kid knows we love them – despite anything they may have done – and then to understand them. And then to apologise too. It's important to start a sin conversation with us talking about our sin, rather than trying to force our children to talk about theirs. Talking about sin can feel heavy. If we talk about sin like kicking God in the shins, then we're saying our little bursts of emotion are making the God of the universe angry at us. A better way is to communicate that we're called to be filled with God's love and sometimes we forget that in our emotion. That's not okay, and so we can ask forgiveness from God and from others.

Progress not perfection

I often advocate telling kids: 'I don't expect you to be perfect, and I can't expect me to be perfect because I'm not finished yet, I'm still growing. I'm going to make a lot of mistakes, you're going to make a lot of mistakes, but we get to help each other. That's a wonderful thing.' So when we argue, we've got to have grace: it's progress, not perfection. We don't expect our kids to be perfect next time, we just expect them to try to make progress. Sometimes we'll try something and it won't work – but that's okay because we're on the same team, trying to figure this out together.

Faith arguments

There are two branches here:

- Your child disagrees with the parenting decisions you make as a Christian
- Your child disagrees with your theology

When our children push against our Christian parenting decisions, this offers some of the best parenting opportunities. We want kids to be thinking, 'Is this scriptural? How do I engage with the world?' If we shut down their thinking, the focus of the argument becomes the control we have over them, rather than encouraging them to actually do the thinking we want them to do to figure out what the world is like.

So – once they're old enough to have this kind of two-way argument – invite their views. Let them talk and explain. You can express your concerns – e.g. it's not scriptural; it's not a safe environment – and encourage your child to tell you how their view engages with those concerns. Feel free to put boundaries in, but inviting your child into a discussion means you're on the same team, finding a solution together.

When our kid announces that they're theologically different from us, often our emotions are so high that we stop listening, because we want them to love and know God so much. We have to acknowledge that we're going to be more emotional sometimes about the spiritual, because we know how important it is. Our job is to help our children process – and them having to deal with our emotions is not the best way to help them.

So you can stress to your child that their views are important to you – but that because God and faith are also important to you, there might be some emotion displayed on your face that they just need to ignore! You could use phrases and questions such as:

- Talk to me about this.
- How have you come to this decision?
- That's really interesting, I love how you looked to the Bible for that.
- This is where I am and this is how I discovered that, but I'm really open to learning more. I am a Christian who is constantly holding up my thoughts, behaviours and beliefs to scripture – some things I may be wrong on, and I'm constantly learning.

- Convince me of this, teach me about it.
- I thought about it, wrestled with it, but I think I'm still landing here because of this scripture…
- That's really interesting you said that – I'm going to go away and think about it.

You're not more important than your child – you're co-disciples, and you're creating windows into what it means to be a disciple who's open to processing new information with God.

Follow-up

- 'Sin' (p. 189) chapter
- Rachel Turner, 'Sandpits and sin', **parentingforfaith.org/post/sandpits-and-sin**

Next steps

- What stood out to you from this chapter? Why?
- Think about the last argument you and your kid had. What lay beneath it?
- When there's an argument in your home, what triggers your response? Would you like this to be different?

B

BEDTIME, SLEEP AND NIGHTMARES

RACHEL TURNER, ROBIN BARFIELD AND ANNA HAWKEN

Night

RACHEL S1E85

God made the night and thinks it's good. The creation story tells us God saved the night for something exciting. We can frame how excited we are about the night and what God's going to do while we sleep. We can explore what's good about the dark so our children start to find it interesting, asking, 'What is one really good thing about night-time?' just as they're going to bed.

Even if your child doesn't want you to pray with them, you can still frame where God is and your hopes that they'll find God's goodness as he goes with them into their dreams.

Helping our kids know that God is with them at night

`RACHEL S1E85`

I have a good friend whose children struggled with sleep and bad dreams. They learnt to say Psalm 3:5 every night: 'I lie down and sleep; I wake again, because the Lord sustains me.' They stuck this verse on their beds so they knew, as they went to bed, that God was with them and if they woke up troubled, that's the first thing they saw.

Bible input at bedtime is really helpful. Night-time is when our kids think and rest and dream, so we want that to be more affected by the great joys of the Christian gospel, rather than something on telly or something that happened with their friends that day.

Routine

`RACHEL S3E11`

The following aspects of bedtime routines help in developing a God-connected child.

Connection to you

Several studies confirm that children who feel connected to their parents have a higher rate of long-term faith stability. Their connection to you is a vital part of your ability to coach them in their spiritual life. Building in time to talk about your day, laugh, ask questions and wonder together is a significant part of bedtime – whether it's two minutes, half an hour or whatever you can spare.

Connection to God

Bedtime is a wonderful space for our kids to connect with God; how that looks is up to you. You can read the Bible, worship or pray together and facilitate them to meet with God on their own.

Leaving them with God

Bedtime is often, 'I love you', and then we're out the door, but the next step is leaving them in the room with God. Whether you say, 'Have a good time with God! You chat and catch and have dreams with God – I'll see you in the morning', or enable them to have some time connecting with God alone, after which you come in to give them a next step, they will know that their connection with God can and will continue without you present.

Helping God-connection at bedtime

ROBIN S3E11

We think carefully about what we say regularly to our children at bedtime – the same phrases, to embed certain truths. Perhaps, 'Daddy loves you very much, Mummy loves you very much and Jesus loves you very much as well', and then, 'Jesus, please would X know that you're with them. Would they love and trust you.'

I want them to know that Jesus is with them in their sleep, and that they're dearly loved by us and Jesus. Different parents will choose different emphases, but having the same thing every night helps it to stick in their memories.

Nightmares

RACHEL S3E11

Sometimes we try to explain away nightmares, but that doesn't tend to be helpful. Even if they sound ridiculous during the daytime, nightmares feel very real as your body experiences fear. Our job is to help children understand what's happening, find peace and take control of their minds.

Enabling our kids to voice the dream can help in learning to take thoughts captive (2 Corinthians 10:5). They could visualise putting a box around it or crumpling it up and throwing it away because it doesn't get to live in their head. Then we can help them find peace.

Talking about nightmares as a biological process takes away the mystery. As we sleep, our brain clears the gunk of the day and makes memories. It's pondering, processing and deciding how to connect things together. Sometimes dreams are simply when our brain puts things together in a weird way as it processes. There's no meaning to it, so we don't need to worry about it; it's just our brain doing something funny.

Then we can refocus our brains with something else we want to think about. We can read, listen to music, sing, read Bible stories, bring up memories and begin to help our brain process all the joyful bits of our day. In putting kids to sleep again, we can ask God to go with them into their dreams; he is not limited by biology or consciousness.

Navigating our children's nightmares is not so much about preventing something bad happening but reconnecting into peace when it does happen.

Nightmares

ANNA S1E34

If your child is experiencing nightmares, ask some trusted friends to pray for them. Be specific, so they know how to pray.

Next, give your child tools for when they're scared. Three different ones are suggested in the 'Scared of the dark' series on the Parenting for Faith website. For my niece, telling stories to God helped her be free of nightmares and was a significant part of her faith journey. These tools can be powerful not just for combating nightmares but also for the rest of their life and faith journey. Finally, *Comfort in the Darkness* is a helpful book to try reading with your child before bed.

Follow-up

- parentingforfaith.org/topics/bedtime
- parentingforfaith.org/post/scared-of-the-dark-helping-our-children-through-the-night
- Rachel Turner, *Comfort in the Darkness: Helping children draw close to God through biblical stories of night-time and sleep* (BRF Ministries, 2016)

Next steps

- Do you have a bedtime routine? What ideas from here might you incorporate to help your children know who God is at night?
- If your children are older, how could you help them know truths about God, night-time and sleep?
- Are any of the ideas about coping with nightmares helpful? Think about what you'll say next time your kid has a nightmare, so you remember what to do when you're half asleep!

B

BIBLE

HELPING OLDER KIDS ENGAGE WITH IT

OLLY GOLDENBERG, RACHEL TURNER
AND BECKY SEDGWICK

Equipping kids to find answers in the Bible

OLLY S1E56

First, show your children how you find answers in the Bible. When I'm read-ing the Bible and there's a verse that stands out and I get all excited about it, I share it with my kids. When someone else is excited, it's infectious for you – so that's led my children to wanting to find out what the Bible says for themselves. So we make regular Bible reading a pattern in our family.

Secondly, create windows into how *you* find answers – for example, 'I was struggling with this, and I went to the Lord and prayed about it, and this is the verse that came to me. This is how I'm chewing it over…' So we're framing things in terms of scripture.

Thirdly, we can sit with our children when they're going through something and show them how the Bible relates to what they're going through. If they're being bullied, we can look at passages that talk about loving your enemies and doing good to those who hurt you. Those aren't easy verses, yet when we have scripture as our foundation, it becomes a life force to us. We're tapping into what God has for us and so our children grow through that – even though it may seem hard at the time.

Then ask questions that prompt them towards Bible stories they know. 'Have you found a verse that helps you? Can you think of a story of anyone else who felt like everyone was against them? Or maybe even wild lions were against them? You're going into the lion's den in your school, aren't you, with the way people are treating you? What happened there?' 'Oh, I know Daniel!'

The next stage is when they come to us and bring such revelation from scripture because they're digging for themselves. It gets even more exciting when it's not just about *their* needs, but they're looking to see how God's word can help *others* with what they're going through.

Sometimes we think our children won't engage with scripture because they tried it before and it was boring, but if we get them enthusiastic about it because of our way of pulling insights out of it, they're going to pick up on this. And when they start to run with it for themselves, when they have a need, they'll know where to turn.

Helping kids love the Bible

RACHEL S1E111

If we only give our children experiences of God but nothing to root them in, it all becomes experiential. God-connected isn't the opposite of God-smart, it's an extension of it. We can help our kids learn how to root themselves in scripture by:

1 Creating windows into how we read scripture and apply it to life.
2 Framing how we can nail down life's experiences to the Bible.
3 Equipping them to learn how to find what they need.
4 Creating opportunities to know and love the Bible – perhaps by finding a verse or story together in scripture that is appropriate to a big family decision.

Framing the Bible's origins

RACHEL S1E14

How did all the different books of the Bible come together? After Jesus' ascension, when his followers were scattered across many different countries, they began to write letters to each other to encourage and give wisdom.

Between 400 and 100BC, the Jewish people had decided what their scriptures were made up of, so the Old Testament was pretty solid for the early church. But there are over 70 pieces of writing that claim to be gospels, and some vastly contradict each other. Around AD100 the early church fathers began to refine scripture. By AD397, councils were establishing criteria for what to include. You could ask your child what criteria they'd use.

They decided on three criteria:

1 Was it written by people who actually knew Jesus?
2 Was it consistent with the Old Testament?
3 Is it in general use by churches all over?

The book of Revelation came a bit later – it got solidified around AD500.

As you pick up storybook Bibles with your kids, you can say how grateful you are for the hundreds of years of wise people praying and putting it together so that we can read God's words.

Understanding the whole story of the Bible

BECKY S2E1

The Bible is big.

It's got everything we need: wisdom, guidance, theology and history, and it helps us understand who God is and who we are – but it can be confusing. We want our kids to learn to access it, but how do we help them make sense of it?

There's something we can do which I've found incredibly helpful: *tell the whole story*. Within the many stories in the Bible, there is one whole story. Once we understand that, the world makes a lot of sense. Here are the six points of the overarching story of the whole Bible:

1 God is love, and he made us out of his great love.
2 People walked away from God, so the world is now totally messed up.
3 Jesus cleared a way for us to be close to God again.
4 God is active in the world and we can partner with him to transform it.
5 God gives us power through his Holy Spirit to join in with his work.
6 One day, it will all be the way God meant it to be forever.

The whole story is simple enough for the smallest child to understand – and it's the story that helps us answer really big questions.

For example, if a child says, 'If God loves me, how come he let Grandma get ill?', instead of having to wade into the theology of suffering, we can frame our answer using the big story. You can say 'Well, we know that God loves us. He loves you, and he loves Grandma. But the world's broken – and bad things happen. We can pray for Grandma, hug her, help her with things she can't do. And whatever happens, we know that one day the world and everyone in it will be exactly back as God wanted it to be forever – including Grandma.'

Follow-up

- 'Bible – helping younger children love it' (p. 27) and 'Bible – the tricky bits' (p. 31) chapters
- **childrencan.co.uk** (Olly Goldenberg)
- **parentingforfaith.org/topics/bible**
- **parentingforfaith.org/post/telling-the-whole-story-facebook-live**
- **parentingforfaith.org/post/telling-bible-stories-well**

Next steps

- How does your child or teen currently engage with the Bible? Do they have questions or assumptions that may colour their view of it?
- How could you create windows into and frame the power of the Bible for you?
- Do you think your kid knows the whole story of the Bible? How could you help them see it?

B

BIBLE
HELPING YOUNGER CHILDREN LOVE IT

JOY WENDLING, RACHEL TURNER AND ED DREW

Exploring the Bible through play

JOY S3E1

Play is important when we are bringing faith to our kids because God wants to draw us to himself, and he's created little brains to grow through play, which increases their curiosity. I can't think of something I want my kids to be curious about more than God and the Bible!

For example, if you're reading the story of Peter walking on water, you could jump on the couch and ask, 'How do you think Peter got out of the boat? Did he jump?', and you can jump off the couch with your kids. 'Or was he more timid, maybe just dipping a little toe in first?' and you all climb back on the couch and cautiously dip your toe on to the carpet. Once he's on the water: 'How did he walk? Did he slide his feet?' and you slide around the living room. 'Or was he stomping on the water, trying to see how big a splash he could make?' and you stomp around. Just being part of the story is how my girls like to experience Bible play.

Play is going to help the story become part of their brain architecture, going from their heads to their hearts. It's going to give them a feeling of enjoyment. When they're teenagers and reading the story of Peter, they'll remember, 'We jumped off the couch with Mum and splashed all through the living room with Jesus.'

It's just about using what you already have as you pick up the Bible and explore together.

I don't think we have to be worried about not getting through the whole story, as it can act like a cliffhanger so your kids will be eager to come back and explore the rest of the story. There shouldn't be any pressure when we read the Bible to our kids. We just do what we can and let the Holy Spirit fill in the rest.

Play builds relationships, so Bible play with my kids is an opportunity for us to build a relationship together and an opportunity for the Holy Spirit to seek out my child. Then it's less pressure for me, because I'm just introducing my kid to a new friend – and that's the opportunity we have in reading the Bible with our kids.

My tips for Bible play:

1   Find a good children's Bible and use the pictures if it has them, before you even read a word. Ask questions like: 'Who do you see in this picture? Who do you think the story's about?' Even silly questions like: 'If this woman wasn't riding a donkey, what other animal could she be riding? Maybe a giraffe?' You're opening their imagination to the story and setting the scene.

2 Look for emotions in the stories. Ask your kids what different people might be feeling and act them out. 'Why did Zacchaeus want to climb the tree? He was curious maybe... what does curiosity look like?' Emotions are a great social and emotional learning opportunity for our kids.

3 The weather! There are lots of stories about weather, and it can be a fun one because it's so experiential. Think about the storm on the boat, rocking back and forth on the sea. Or if you're in the desert, what does that feel like? Act out those little things and it will become experiential.

I can't control whether my kids choose to follow God when they grow up, but what I can control right now is the environment and the way I present it. If God is someone who is engaging and fun to be with – which I believe he is – then for me 'success' is presenting him as authentically as I can to my kids and enjoying that time together.

When kids don't want to listen to Bible stories

RACHEL S1E69

We want our kids to listen to Bible stories, but sometimes they don't find them interesting. Most kids' books are so targeted to what children love that Bible stories might not seem as fun as other books. That's okay because the Bible, although wonderful, wasn't written to be the best children's book ever.

Here are three ideas that may help your kids engage better:

- Starting with the Bible story means you can start with the truth of who God is and then ease into funny stories that aren't real. You're also starting off with them at their most settled, so if they're going to get wriggly it'll be in somebody else's book.
- Change whose job it is to pick the Bible story, so it becomes something you do as a family. You can ask why they picked that story, and their answer might be an interesting way of showing how Bible stories are relevant to everyday life.
- Try swapping the time of day you read the Bible together, taking it out of the category of bedtime entertainment.

Engaging kids with the Bible

`ED S4E8`

People can assume that opening a Bible with children has to be well behaved, ordered and like church. That's an unfair expectation, and it's usually why people don't open the Bible with their children.

So the first thing is: when you open your Bible with children, it's chaotic and messy, but we still think it's worth doing. You don't have to have all the answers. The Lord has us and our children. Make it short; ask them questions; allow them to engage; allow them to play; get the toys out; work it through together; make it less than ten minutes; pray at the end and talk to God about what you've learned.

Children look to their parents for what they get excited about. So if we're intimidated, baffled or bored, our children will be too. As the parent, you're the best person in the world to teach the tricky bits of the Bible because your children know you love them and they trust you. You know what frightens them, what they don't understand, what they're ready for, what they're not ready for – you are the world expert on your children. Tread carefully, but don't be afraid – be confident. If you get it wrong, give them a big hug and come back to it in a year's time.

Follow-up

- 'Bible – helping older children engage with it' (p. 22) and 'Bible – the tricky bits' (p. 31) chapters
- **parentingforfaith.org/topics/bible**
- **createdtoplay.com** (Joy Wendling)
- **faithinkids.org** (Ed Drew)

Next steps

- Do your kids engage with the Bible at the moment? How do they do that?
- What ideas from this chapter might you want to try?
- There are many Bible storybooks out there. Could you swap books with other families so you can try some different ones from time to time?

B

BIBLE
THE TRICKY BITS

RACHEL TURNER

Bible baddies

RACHEL S1E71

Sometimes we find the 'bad guy' Bible stories interesting because of the conflict and eventual defeat. Often, we identify with the good guy. But that only gives us access to half the story, because there's something powerful about seeing ourselves in the bad guy too: learning why they, beloved child of God, made choices against God's will. It's powerful to talk about the bad guys not as irreparable, irredeemable people, but as people who God loved deeply, who were walking separate from him.

Take Saul: he didn't want to be king but finally stepped up – and then became this controlling power-hungry person, more concerned about other people's opinions than what God was saying to him. The Bible says the Holy Spirit left him and he didn't even notice. I never want to be so worried about keeping my job that I lose what God is saying to me. There is so much we can learn from people in the Bible. When the Bible talks about Pharaoh hardening his heart, that concept of having a soft or hard heart is helpful: how do we keep our hearts soft towards other people and God?

There is richness in seeing ourselves in the people who are bringing conflict in scripture. When are we blind to injustice? When are we perpetrating oppression on somebody else? When are we the bully or the one falsely teaching? We are faulty human beings – and if we begin to talk about the Bible 'bad guys' with compassion and understanding, then it helps our kids see that scripture has something to say to them when they make mistakes.

As you read Bible stories together, ask your kids questions about the baddies of the Bible, such as: 'How did God feel about those people?', 'Why do you think they did that?', 'Do you ever think like that? I know I do…' Looking at the people who weren't walking with God is as powerful as looking at the ones who were, adding a richness to how we look for God and what he's telling us in scripture.

Tricky biblical love stories

RACHEL S1E17

The biblical love stories in the Old Testament are not the ideal!

Take Isaac and Rebekah (Genesis 24): when it was time for Isaac to get married, a servant went to find him a wife. The servant didn't want to make the wrong decision, so told God a sentence that he wanted the right woman to say, and watched to see who God picked. Rebekah came out and said the words, so the servant went to her house, spoke to her father who agreed, then Rebekah and Isaac got married.

Then there was Jacob and Rachel (Genesis 29): Jacob worked for Laban for seven years because he liked Rachel and wanted to marry her. (It says nothing about whether or not Rachel liked Jacob.) But at the last minute, Laban gave Jacob his elder daughter Leah. Laban told Jacob he could have Rachel if he worked another seven years, and Jacob agreed.

Meanwhile, Esther (Esther 2) was plucked from nowhere and brought to the king's palace, where she was paraded around and eventually picked to marry King Xerxes.

So how do we talk about them with our kids?

We tend to either skip over these stories or brush them off as 'a different time'. But all of scripture is useful for correction, instruction and teaching, so one question to ask as you're reading these stories is: 'Where is God in this story?' These stories don't look the way we would necessarily want to have our lives play out – so where is God in that? You can talk about God listening to the heartfelt cry of Isaac wanting to find the right partner, or God being in the middle of weaving together Jacob and Rachel's families to create Jesus' family line, or God using Esther to save the world in a marriage that she wouldn't have chosen for herself. God is in everybody's story, no matter what it looks like.

Another thing to talk about is the character of these women. At the time, women didn't get to choose who they married – but they did choose how they responded to their situation. We can see real strength of character, grace and humility in these women. How do you do that? How do you position your heart to serve and love your family when it isn't the situation you would have chosen? We can talk about how there are many scenarios in relationships that we wouldn't have picked – how do we persevere? You could even talk about how marriages sometimes still work like that, around the world, in terms of arranged marriages or women not having a choice, and what that looks like for them and for justice. If appropriate for your children, you could talk about how sometimes relationships can be abusive, and that no one should be made to feel they have to persevere in an abusive relationship.

It's also interesting looking at their life stories after they get married, such as the fertility struggles of Rachel and Leah and the fighting between them. It could be an interesting opening to talk about sibling rivalry and how you feel when somebody else has more or is more special to somebody.

How do you explain concubines to kids?

RACHEL S1E44

In biblical times, thousands of years ago, one person could have multiple wives. Back then, women died a lot in childbirth because they didn't have the medical advances we have now. If men were going to have families that grew and continued, having one wife at a time could have been a problem.

You can explain that sometimes it's just how culture developed. Men used to be the most important, and women were expendable, so it was all about the man's needs and wants. If he wanted lots of children, then he would have multiple wives, because back then it was all about the man and not about what the woman wanted.

What we value in our culture today is that one person can be with another person, and they can be the best minister of God to that person. Dedicating ourselves to one person shows us a bit of God's heart for us; it shows us that we can take care of someone and not hurt them. It's saying: 'You are the most important person to me, and I'm going to sacrifice for you so that together we can experience something of God's sacrifice and connection with us.'

Follow-up

- 'Bible – helping older kids engage with it' (p. 22) and 'Big questions' (p. 35) chapters
- parentingforfaith.org/topics/bible

Next steps

- Do your kids ask questions about the Bible? If not, how could you open up conversations about what they are reading or hearing?
- What have you learned from Bible baddies? Could you create windows into that for your child?
- Are there other parts of the Bible that you find tricky? Who or what could help you figure them out?

B

BIG QUESTIONS

JUSTIN BRIERLEY, J.JOHN, BECKY SEDGWICK,
ANNA HAWKEN AND RACHEL TURNER

Asking questions

JUSTIN S6E3

Asking questions is a brilliant way of helping people to understand. The worst thing is to close down the question just because you don't have the answers. This sends a message that Christianity can't cope with real life – and that's false. It's important that our young people know we want to engage their questions and at the very least try to search for answers.

'I don't know' is a perfectly valid answer, and kids appreciate the truthfulness of that. But then look into it together. We're there to try to help our kids flourish and hopefully step into their own faith. Perhaps we've never thought about these questions, but nonetheless we need to be prepared to help our kids navigate them.

There's lots we're not going to know: we are finite human minds talking about the greatest mystery. To have faith is to say: 'I've seen enough about God that I'm prepared to live in the tension of the things I don't know.'

Prayer is where you can give questions to God. You can talk about them – but in prayer we admit our limits, saying, 'I don't have the answers but we're giving this to God.' You're not going to get every question answered, but you have security that God is there and listening.

Discernment is important. We can give our kids a groundwork of the core aspects of Christianity and how to spot things that don't conform. But then give them the opportunity to engage with other voices, and hopefully you're continuing the conversation as they do that. We're all in the process of growing.

Big questions

J.JOHN S8E8

If we could understand God, he would be the same as our little minds and therefore not worth believing in. We live in a world of miracle and mystery, and you've somehow got to hold the two together. But there is enough out there to illuminate our thinking and our hearts.

When faced with big questions, my approach would be three things:

1 **Praying.** Pray that the Lord will open the eyes of those who are asking.
2 **Caring.** Little people don't care how much we know until they know how much we care. Am I hearing not just the question but what's behind the question? How do we address both question and *questioner*?
3 **Sharing.** It's not just communicating belief, but modelling the way we live. One of the things we exposed our children to, growing up, was other Christians in our home and we'd have fascinating conversations which included our children.

Our children are often in toxic environments, and sometimes we are almost oblivious to that. How do we help our children filter what's going through? Maybe we need to explain what we do. 'I read the Bible because it's a filter. There's so much that's out in the world and the only way I can filter it is through the Bible.'

We also need to communicate with our children. How are they finding things? Are they struggling? Do they have questions? It's healthy to have good conversations with our children; there might come a time when they don't want to, but if they do, then we should welcome it.

Are answers important?

BECKY S1E114

The Sticky Faith research suggests that one thing which helps children retain their faith once they leave home is having answers to their questions. But a young adult told me recently that what helped her faith to 'stick' was having a safe space to ask any question.

So maybe the question is: how important is it that we *make space* for the questions kids have about God?

Trying to answer questions puts massive pressure on us as parents/carers because it means we need to know the answers. But making space for questions – anyone can do that.

When God doesn't make sense, that's okay – because he's too big for me to make sense of. I know God well enough to trust that when I don't understand, it's still okay.

Big questions are vital because our kids are immersed in a culture that ridicules God or explains him badly. Daily, they see and hear people who think the Bible is just a collection of fairy stories, and they'll also have experiences which will make them doubt. But they're not necessarily looking for a theological answer; they're trying to figure out how you can reconcile these things and still be a Christian.

There are three things we can do easily to help them:

1 Make space for questions and encourage debate – no question about God is off limits.
2 As you talk, include your experience of God. Share stories of times you've dealt with big questions, and how you still know he's a good God.
3 When you don't know the answer, talk about what you *do* know. I don't

know why God allowed me to suffer, but I do know that he comforted me. That's an incredibly important two-sided sentence: 'I don't know this... but I do know that.'

Most kids are just looking for ways to help them navigate those unexpected bumps in the road on their journey with Jesus. By a safe space to ask and debate, you're enabling them to be comfortable with the answer 'I don't know'.

Four steps to answering any question

ANNA S2E5

Whatever age they are, children will ask us questions – often ones that we don't immediately know the answer to and often at an inconvenient time! Here are four steps that can help:

1 **Ask: 'What do you think?'** They'll often tell you more about why they're asking the question, where they got the idea or what stirred it.
2 **Ask: 'What do we know?'** We might not have the full answer, but what things do we know for certain? Is there a relevant Bible verse or story?
3 **Ask: 'What do we not know?'** We don't need to pretend we have all the answers or make things up. Get kids and teens comfortable with sitting with the things we don't know.
4 **Share how you've handled it.** The amazing privilege of a child/teen asking a question is not in just giving them an answer, but in creating windows into how you've handled this in life.

Apologetics

RACHEL S3E2

How do you handle it when a fact comes in that challenges what you think about the Bible? If a child has a constantly curious mind, we need to teach them how to walk alongside it, because no matter how many apologetics they're given, there will be more questions.

You could use statements and questions such as:

- What an interesting fact! Show me the article that came from.
- How interesting! I wonder what it says…
- How do we know what the Bible says is accurate? What does that look like?
- How do biblical theologians and archaeologists date things from scripture?
- How do other scholars interpret this?
- Is there more research we could consider?
- How does this journey/answer impact your relationship with God?

Be ready to explore their ideas. Teach them how to hold this approach as part of a normal journey with God. Frame how sometimes new facts will make us question things – and on that journey, we can sit with God and ask him to show us his truth.

Curious questions help us see God in a new way. I encourage you to disciple your kid in the process of curiosity so it's not just about what's going on in their head but how that impacts their heart.

Follow-up

- 'Doubt' (p. 70), 'RE lessons' (p. 166) and 'Bible – the tricky bits' (p. 31) chapters
- Sticky Faith research: **fulleryouthinstitute.org/stickyfaith**
- **parentingforfaith.org/post/questions**
- **parentingforfaith.org/post/intellectual-wrestlers-equipping-kids-who-need-to-know**
- **justinbrierley.com**
- **canonjjohn.com**

Next steps

- Do your kids know it's okay to ask any question about faith and God?
- How could you create a culture of asking and exploring questions together in your home?
- Do your kids have big questions? What might help them to explore them?

CHRISTMAS

RACHEL TURNER AND LIZZIE LAFERTON

A 'should-free' Christmas

RACHEL S1E52

Every year, Christian parents are surrounded by endless opportunities to embrace the spiritual focus of Christmas: Advent calendars, devotionals, services, books. But there is no Christmas 'should': no one right way to do Christmas.

You may be having a rough year and barely have money or time to engage. You may have kids for whom a season of sensory overload is a hard slog. Your children may struggle with earlier memories of Christmas. You may be suffering loss or just extreme sleep deprivation.

An excellent spiritual parent is someone who proactively walks alongside their children and helps them meet and know God. They authentically let their children see into their lives and help them connect with God for themselves.

You don't have to do a Jesse tree or go to every Christmas service. Feel free to be you in this season, because if God is in the ordinary, boring bits of life, then he is right there with you, whatever it looks like. You can help your kids find him there. Jesus came to be 'God with us' in our circumstances and with the capabilities we have right now.

Which nativity character is your child?

RACHEL S1E53

Every child is different, and knowing what makes them tick will help you see how best to help them meet and know God this season.

Mary was told who Jesus was, but it was nine months before she met him. Some of our kids are like that: God is faithful in engaging with them, but they're on a slow burn of getting to know him. With this type of kid, **framing** is useful because it helps them see where God is in their lives and how they can begin to recognise him.

Elizabeth recognised God in others. Her baby sensed Jesus, and the Holy Spirit confirmed it to her. Some kids recognise something of God in their parents or others. The more we can **create windows** into our lives, the more we create opportunities for our children to see God.

The shepherds met God through a supernatural encounter which made them run towards Jesus. Some kids have big experiences which lead them straight to God. **Chat and catch** creates space for this. Play worship music, invite God to lie down with you as you go to sleep, light a candle. If your kid has had an encounter with God, continue to create space for them to meet with God.

The wise men studied, sacrificed, travelled, investigated – and discovered Jesus at the end of a long search. I know kids who've wrestled with the idea of God and Jesus. When they find Jesus, they are rock solid. **Unwinding** helps. If your kid thinks deeply, grab some apologetics books, watch videos or listen to podcasts, and join them in the wrestling.

Simeon and Anna were at the temple with eager hearts, ready to respond when they encountered God at work. God is talking to our kids; they're processing what's happening in scripture and so – like Simeon and Anna – when Jesus comes across their path, they want to respond. You can help: this is **surfing the waves**.

Connecting with God at Christmas

LIZZIE S4E10

Traditions are our friends at Christmas. We can make the most of those things we'll be doing anyway, tweaking them to give a Christ-focus among the busyness.

Look for times in your day when you read stories. Younger children often have stories before bed. School-aged kids might have reading to do at home. If we're going to read anyway, let's read the Christmas story.

Could our decorations include 'Immanuel', 'Jesus Christ' or the names in Isaiah 9?

There's more shopping in December. We can pray before we go, asking God to give us what we need and, afterwards, thanking him for what he gave us – even if it wasn't what we were hoping to find. We can talk about God being the provider, the one who gives good gifts.

As we open our Advent calendars, we thank God for a gift he's given us. On the second day we'll look for two and on the third day, three and so on.

When we turn the Christmas tree lights on, we could learn a memory verse like: 'The people walking in darkness have seen a great light' (Isaiah 9:2) or 'I am the light of the world' (John 8:12). It's finding little moments where you don't need to do *more*, but just slightly *differently,* to keep Jesus central.

Jesus shows us giving that is humble, need-meeting, sacrificial. We can encourage our children both to *look* at Christ as the giver and *imitate* Christ as the giver. When our kids were very small, they had no money but could make presents: bookmarks, paperweights, baking – learning they were gift-givers, not just getters.

Engaging with the Christmas story with a young child might involve props, playing, acting. With tweens and teens there are devotionals and retellings that help them to see what the story reveals about God.

Thinking about the ordinariness of Mary and the shepherds can help children see the relevance of it to them. Ordinary people got invited to be part of something extraordinary and we're invited too.

Older kids might think about emotions: how scary it must have been for Mary and Joseph, the scorn they would have been subjected to. You could talk about what they knew about God that helped them have peace and trust him in challenging circumstances.

You might talk about the social context Jesus was born into: injustice, poverty, political oppression – celebrating the fact that Jesus came for the humble and the outsider. Children know what it's like to fear being powerless and excluded, and this story shouts about the God who sees and cares, and who invites us all to come and know Christ.

Follow-up

- 'Advent' (p. 10) and 'Santa' (p. 168) chapters
- The Bible Project: **bibleproject.com**
- Lizzie Laferton, *The God of Amazing Gifts* (The Good Book Company, 2022)
- **parentingforfaith.org/topics/advent-and-christmas**

Next steps

- Do you feel any particular 'shoulds' at Christmas? What would you prefer Christmas to be like?
- Which nativity character most reminds you of your child(ren) at the moment?
- How could you create one or two opportunities for your kids to engage with who God is in the Christmas season?

C

CHURCH
HELPING KIDS
ENGAGE WITH IT

JOSH LEES AND RACHEL TURNER

When your teenager is disengaged with church

JOSH S1E14

Ask why they don't want to come to church. Reasons could include:

- It might be the things they find boring are things you find boring.
- It might be they have serious questions about God and faith that are

not being discussed. Providing a place for questions to be engaged with seriously is important.

- It might be they don't have friends their own age.

Sometimes we can find a youth group that our young people can join. Sometimes it's about encouraging them to press on. Life in community is hard, and all of us struggle with church at different points. We can support our teenagers in seeing church as something they are part of as well, encouraging them in the contribution they make.

There were only two other kids in my church: my siblings. It was tough. But my parents made space to take us to youth clubs and events that we could connect with. They talked about the services with us at home and asked questions that were on our level. We also found that, even though there weren't any other kids, some of the adults started to look out for us. We respected them, and they felt more like family in the end. I look back fondly on those years.

Not having church friends their own age doesn't have to doom our teenagers. It's harder, and it's fine to be honest about that, but it's not a barrier.

Extra-curricular activities

RACHEL S5E11

When extra-curricular activities clash with church, the challenge is the competing values of wanting to see them flourish in things they love and wanting to see them flourish in their faith by being part of a faith community.

The question is: 'What is most important about church? Why is church important to us?' Almost everything we do with our kids is not just for now, but the future; we want to give them a framework to make those decisions about church for themselves at some point.

Your values might be different, but mine would focus around community, challenge and service. I would ask:

- Where will our child commit to a Jesus-loving community?
- Where will they be challenged?
- Where are they going to serve?

Some teenagers might commit to an adult home group on a weeknight, listen weekly to a challenging podcast and serve in the Saturday morning older people's breakfast. Fantastic! They are accessing church. You're then figuring out *together* how to connect with church and discipling your child in the 'why' of church.

When your child doesn't like *your* church

RACHEL S5E11

In session 8 of the Parenting for Faith course, we talk about church being a place where we:

- are encouraged and encourage others
- are loved and love others
- connect with God
- are part of the body of Christ
- are being transformed.

If your kid feels like none of those values are happening for them at your current church, discuss whether you value going to the same church or not. For some families it's important, while other families are happy to facilitate everyone going to different churches.

Teaching our kids *how* to make decisions about church is important. It's about values and your approach to worship, not style, because you can connect with God anywhere.

Finding a church when they leave home

RACHEL S5E11

It's helpful to have conversations about what church is for, and that no church is going to be perfect or make you happy all the time. Look together at different local churches to see what they're like, how they're different and what you think you'd like about each one.

When you are looking at where your teen might move away to – whether it's university, vocational school, a job or moving to be with their friend – look at churches as part of the consideration. This then becomes part of the package. Whether or not your kid accesses it, they know where it is, they've already had introductions and been to a service.

If our kids are only used to one church, it's a big leap to pick a new one. So give them experiences of walking into a different worshipping space and spotting the similarities. Knowing we can be comfortable in different churches is a great skill to give kids.

When *you* don't like church

RACHEL S5E11

How you speak about church and its people informs your child's view, not only of that church but of all churches. We adults can sometimes hold nuances that children can't. That doesn't mean you always have to be positive, but be aware that any time you talk about things you don't like, our children are listening and curating a catalogue of why this place is unsafe, stressful or untrustworthy.

Either don't debrief in front of them or frame it well. For example, you could say: 'There are some changes happening and I'm not great with change. I need to decide: do I need to change my heart? Or do I need to learn new things? Or is it wrong?' It's okay to be critical and have robust conversations. At some point, they may be stressed with church, and it's important to frame a healthy way of engaging with it.

Sometimes we come home from church frustrated, and we explode. It's okay to say, 'I don't think that was a healthy way of processing my frustration', explaining that church is a place of broken people who are still figuring it out.

If you're struggling with church right now, consider what healthy way you want your kids to have in their head of how to process it, so that if and when they hit that bump in the future, they don't assume the answer is to leave.

Follow-up

- 'Church hurt' (p. 49) and both 'Disengagement' (p. 64, p. 67) chapters
- Session 8 of the Parenting for Faith course: **parentingforfaith.org/course**
- Session 5 of the Parenting Teens course: **parentingforfaith.org/course/session-5-teenagers-and-church**
- **parentingforfaith.org/post/connecting-with-church-and-additional-needs-faqs**
- **parentingforfaith.org/post/summary-helping-kids-engage-with-church**

Next steps

- Why is church important to you?
- What does your child or teen like about church? What do they not like?
- What would you like your child to know and feel about church when they leave home?

CHURCH HURT

NATALIE THOMAS RUNION, ROSIE BOOTHER AND HEIDI BOOTHER

When church lets us down

NATALIE S7E8

Church hurt can occur because of the church's inability to have the hard conversations. When our kids start to ask hard questions, the church sends them back into the world to discover the answers. As a church, we need to be better at responding to those questions with biblical wisdom and discernment.

Church hurt can also occur when we don't make space for children to use their giftings. There's no junior Holy Spirit – so when our children show us a gifting in worship leading, speaking, art or kindness, we can start calling that out. Giving children the opportunity to use their God-given gifts is a beautiful way to include them in the church.

When our children have been hurt by church, we have two options: gaslight them or listen to them. When we say, 'Unpack that for me, tell me exactly what was said and who said it', we can start to process it together. Rather than trying to defend the church, be your child's greatest advocate as a good listener. As they begin to process, we have to slow ourselves down, not being offended by what happened to our child, but spending time praying with them, without trying to rush a healing or defend a church that may truly have hurt them.

Listening is a primary ministry for parents. I'm learning too that children have an ability to forgive much quicker than us – so they will, in turn, minister to us as we are ministering to them.

Christians panic when they see the word 'deconstruction', but if your child or teen tells you they're deconstructing their faith, listen. They are unwinding the 'religion' that has been placed on them by the church. Deconstruction can be healthy when we have a framework around us to re-build. Look at the Bible, see what Jesus said and internalise the truth of who Jesus says we are by his word, not the religion that has been put on us through the church.

When it comes to healing from church trauma or religious abuse, having biblical counselling gives us a safe space to unpack things that have happened to us. God is not in a hurry with our healing. It may take some time to start to see the church as something other than a place that caused us pain, rather than a place to bring us back into relationship with God and his people. We would rather our children take their time in healing than rush them and have them get hurt again. When we're healed, we can put up healthy boundaries that help us not get unnecessarily hurt again. Healing is not linear, and God heals us all differently, so be patient.

I had it rooted in me from a young age that if I prayed, God would hear me. So when the church hurt me, I had to trust that the God of the Bible was going to be the God I could cry out to. My parents also did a good job of trusting other people to nurture my faith. There were people in my life who knew Jesus and knew our family, who'd pray for me, help me unpack my thoughts and told me when I wasn't believing the word of God. It's about daily showing up and saying, 'Even when people fail me, God is still good and he doesn't change.'

Leaving church

As we watched friends gradually leave church, we framed it for our children in terms of them having fallen out with the church, not with us. 'They don't agree with everything that's going on, but we feel God wants us to stay; we just have to love a little more.'

It was incredibly hard. Your church is your family, and ours was all our kids had ever known. The pain was huge. But there was always discussion, which was helpful.

When we eventually left, it was a discussion the whole way through. What parts don't you agree with? Why are we doing this? We're not always going to get things right. The church is like anywhere else: we make mistakes, we don't communicate, love or forgive as we should. God's desire is for us to work within that, but we're human and we sin.

There were lots of conversations about forgiveness. Seeing the damage that had been done, our kids were quite angry. They didn't understand why something so loving had become a cause of pain. The forgiveness they'd been taught was now having to come into practice.

We always took it back to God. We still believe in God. God is the same today as he was – but as a church, we're human and we fail.

We didn't hide our hurt, because in life there will be hard times and we wanted to show our kids how we deal with that. There were times when it affected our mood because it was all-consuming. I had to change my job. I believe in reconciliation so just presumed that I wouldn't leave a church. I wish we hadn't all had to go through that, but it did strengthen our family unit, because it was something that we had to do together. As our children have got older, we've shared more with them – not everything, but when it applies to their lives, such as how they might deal with the different people they come into contact with.

Follow-up

- 'Church – helping kids engage with it' (p. 44) and both 'Disengagement' (p. 64, 67) chapters
- natalierunion.com
- parentingforfaith.org/post/summary-church-struggles

Next steps

- What stood out to you from this chapter for your family?
- How can you help your kids understand that while churches might fail us, God doesn't?
- Do your kids have other adults in their lives who will help nurture their faith?

DEATH AND BEREAVEMENT

ABIGAIL RICHARDSON, JAMES YEATES, ANNIE WILLMOT AND ANNA HAWKEN

Framing death for children

ABIGAIL S7E15

Very young children communicate a lot through play, so you might notice that after bereavement they play differently. Look at their body language or behaviour changes. Consider how they've reacted to everyday transitions, as then you'll see how to communicate in a way that is unique to them.

Allow your child to see you grieving. How you take that grief to the Lord is going to help your child see how they can too. You can say that something very sad has happened and our emotions are dealing with it in different ways, so rather than hitting your brother, what can we do with all that energy that would allow us to be angry, but not to sin?

Psalm 46 reminds us that God is our present help in time of need, right there in our pain. What can we do with our sadness? Take it to the Lord. Children might want to draw or write some of the memories that the Lord allowed them to enjoy together.

It's in moments of suffering that we get to lean close to the Lord and help our children see God in that. Explain it's okay to cry or not cry, and that the process may be long, but we're not doing it on our own if we're in the Lord.

What does our hope in Jesus mean in a time when we're suffering like this? Ultimately, Jesus came to bring an end to sin and death. There is going to be a day where our tears will be wiped away, so we can grieve with that hope, showing our children the difference that being a believer makes.

Where are they now?

JAMES S1E35

What I tell children is the same thing I tell adults: ultimately no living person on this earth can be the judge of what happens to a person when they die. We get some indications through the Bible, for example, 'My Father's house has many rooms' (John 14:2). But only God truly knows the decisions that a person made in their life and when they finally met him.

We know that God is a God of love. He cares for us and wants the best for us. If we believe this, then we need to learn to trust that God has our friends and family in his loving care. The wider ramifications of how we respond to Christ are more for us to discern as adults, not something I would burden a child with; rather, I would encourage them to grow to know the God of love who promises to hold all our relatives in his hands.

Helping kids process death

ANNIE S1E56

Be honest. If you're grieving, it's okay to say to your kids, 'I don't know what I'm feeling' or to tell them that you're angry. It's important to show your emotion, because the more you share yours, the more they know it's okay to share theirs.

Accept what they're feeling. If they're crying, let them cry and be with them in their sadness. If they're angry, let them be angry – don't feel you need to fix it.

Avoid euphemisms. Rather than saying grandma 'passed away' or 'went to sleep', say that she died. Children take things literally: if you talk about someone being 'lost' they wonder when they're going to be found, or 'going to sleep' makes them anxious that someone could just go to sleep and not wake up.

Don't be afraid to let your child ask questions and figure out all the bits they need to know. Tell them what you need them to know, then let them lead you if they want more. Often those conversations will happen steadily over time, so invite them to talk if they want to. Children process things in a different way and often they're quick to move on.

Using the Key Tools to prepare a child for a funeral

ANNA S3E8

- **Creating windows.** Show your child how you're processing the grief. For example, I didn't hide when I'd been crying, explaining how I'd been chatting to God about it.
- **Framing.** Before we went to the funeral, we talked about different emotions we might see, about the songs we were going to sing and how people might talk about his life. Afterwards, we talked about what stood out to my child, what she found interesting and how it made her feel about God.

- **Unwinding.** Spot how your child's view of God has been shaped by the bereavement – whether helpfully, in giving them a fuller picture of God, or unhelpfully skewing it.
- **Chat and catch.** We talked to God about how we were feeling and some things that we wanted to pray for the family.
- **Surfing the waves.** For us, there was loads of focus on 'catch' because my daughter liked asking God questions, but we also told God how we were feeling or what we were thinking.

Follow-up

- 'Death of a child or parent' (p. 57) and 'Illness' (p. 110) chapters
- **parentingforfaith.org/post/grief** – includes a list of recommended resources and places to go for support
- **cherishcounsellingpractice.org** (Abigail Richardson)
- 'Home' by Kids Club – an album of Christian songs for families processing bereavement (producer Simon Parry was our guest on S1E39) – **open.spotify.com/album/2lH0YWZoGqUZsmUJ5qX7Rk?si=rk 7l1ZkCQm2T-EqSSoQE3g&nd=1&dlsi=f382c3a95d6641a1**

Next steps

- If your child hasn't yet experienced someone close to them dying, how could you open up conversations about death and dying? What stories could you share of your own experiences and who God was for you at that time?
- If your child is grieving or scared of death, how could you encourage them to connect with God and chat to him about it?
- Are there any biblical truths about death and dying that your child might not know? What might help you lay those foundations of truth for them?

D

DEATH OF A CHILD OR PARENT

REBECCA FOGARTY AND XANTHE BARKER

Losing a child to cancer

REBECCA S9E5

When our first son Leo came along, he wasn't very well. Other mums seemed to be able to do a lot more than I could, and life was hard. When he was about 14 months, having been sick for a long time, we found that he had a rare sarcoma that was growing from his prostate. He nearly died.

They couldn't treat it in our local hospital here in Tasmania, so we had to go to Melbourne, which meant a trip with the air ambulance in the middle of the night. We had nothing but some nappies and a bunny rug – and we didn't go home for seven months. We didn't have any clothes, and my phone broke in the process so I couldn't contact anyone. It was an absolute nightmare, and I learned what it is to feel completely helpless. I couldn't protect my son, and any plan I'd had for my family life was absolutely out of the window.

We moved to Melbourne and stayed in hostel accommodation with 50 other families all going through hell as well. It was incredibly bleak. We felt very alone. But God was right there with us. In the early days, as the most terrible things were happening and it was clear that others just didn't understand my anguish, the Holy Spirit pressed on my heart that other people would never understand, but that he was there with us. I could unburden myself to him as much as I needed to, and he would always understand. That was incredibly comforting.

Eventually we came home and everything looked good; we tried to get back to normal life, but the cancer returned. So it was back to Melbourne again, for another six months, except this time the treatment didn't work, and we were told to take him home to die. All through that, people were praying and miraculously Leo got better. We were told he had weeks left, maybe months – and instead he just recovered. The tumour shrank to almost nothing.

I got pregnant with our second child, but Leo got sick again. This time it felt so fast, and then suddenly he was gone. I call that period of my life 'intermission', when I went from being a mother to not being a mother. Overnight my life changed so much: I lost my son, but I also lost my identity as a hospital mum, which had become my 24–7 job. My friends were the doctors and nurses, and suddenly that was all gone – and I still hadn't finished university, so I didn't have the career that I planned either. It was just black, just nothing.

A lot of people thought, 'At least she's still pregnant – there's another baby coming', but the nine weeks between Leo's death and the birth of our next child was really difficult. I don't know who coordinated it – perhaps it was the Holy Spirit – but the people in my church here at home made sure that a different person took me out for coffee every single day of that nine-week intermission. That was the best therapy I could have asked for, because I could tell my story over and over again. People didn't get bored, and I didn't feel like I was burdening any one person; the community just carried me through that. There was so much grace.

I feel like I've had two families, because one ended before the second one began. We had a miscarriage after Leo, so we had a boy and a girl, then intermission, and another boy and a girl. Intermission gave me an opportunity for reflection which I don't think every parent gets. Now I parent with more urgency, knowing that I don't know how long they're here for or how long I'm here for. But I have 'now', so what can I put into 'now'? I'm also eternity-focused, because that's when we're all going to be together again. We talk about eternity a lot as a family, and my children are very comfortable talking about death and about Leo and about the fact that this life is not permanent. My earthside children look forward to all four of them being together.

Processing the death of a parent

XANTHE S5E9

One way in which my children's faith journey has been affected by their father's death is around unanswered prayer. Loads of people from our church community walked alongside us during Sam's illness. We were all very confident that God could heal Sam – but he didn't. My daughter sometimes feels a bit resentful that God didn't answer that prayer. If people around her are praying for something big, she finds it harder to believe that God will do it.

They're both confident that Sam is in heaven, but when the topic comes up in church or RE lessons, they start thinking about their dad and get sad. My son finds it hard to concentrate because he's so busy thinking about Daddy that he forgets to pay attention to what he's meant to be doing.

It's been important to me to keep the legacy of Sam's faith alive for our children. Sam was always a big advocate of how much Jesus loved a party, so we've carried that on as a family. The kids get that their Daddy's in a great place, having a fun time. Sam was big into hospitality. Hosting a homegroup helps my children realise that part of our faith is opening our home to other people. Sam grew up in a church family and even on holiday they'd go to church, so that's something we've tried to do too.

Follow-up

- 'Death and bereavement' (p. 53) and 'Illness' (p. 110) chapters
- parentingforfaith.org/post/grief

Next steps

- Do you resonate with anything in Rebecca's or Xanthe's stories?
- How might you support someone in a similar situation?
- If your child has experienced the death of a close family member, how has that affected their relationship with God?

D

DISAPPOINTMENT IN GOD

RACHEL TURNER S1E74

When our children reflect on their experiences, one question that may pop up is 'Why didn't God...?' Why didn't God give me what I asked him for? Why doesn't God talk to me?

As parents and carers, we are sometimes fearful of letting our children ask big things of God in case they get disappointed. We don't want them to ask God for the big stuff, because what if God doesn't pull through? We're afraid that their disappointment will become the deal breaker in their relationship with God. I want to talk about how to help your kids through spiritual disappointment so that you're not afraid of it and they're not afraid of it.

Firstly, it's a good thing when our children are disappointed with God when we are around. I'd much rather them experience disappointment when we can walk with them through it than they try to handle it on their own. So when you see your kid being disappointed with God, feel thankful that you get to be here, because this is not the only time they're going to experience it. If we can teach them how to walk through it, we are setting them up for a life of faith, rather than a moment of faith.

Secondly, this experience is an important process of faith. If we can give our kids a framework for this, then they'll know how to walk so much of life with God. So how do we help our kids deal with disappointment, at any age?

- We can create windows of what this looks like for us – telling stories of when we asked God for something and it didn't happen, how we came through it, what that did to our heart and for how long, and how we coped with it.

- We can frame for our kids that it's normal to experience disappointment – that people in the Bible and people we know have dealt with those same feelings.

We don't want to let disappointment rob us of the greatest gift, a life with God, but we do need to learn to deal with those emotions. We see a good three-stage pattern in the Psalms:

1 **Tell God how you feel.** The Psalms show us that when we feel disappointment or confusion, we're supposed to push into God. Psalm 10 starts off with a long, nine-verse rant, which begins: 'Why, Lord, do you stand far off? Why do you hide yourself in times of trouble?' Psalm 88 is another example. To encourage our kids to run *to* God with their feelings, rather than *away* from him, is an incredibly significant move.

2 **Speak truth and thank God.** After we tell God how we feel, it's helpful to remember that although we may might not understand why God's allowed something, or why we don't seem able to hear him – or whatever it is – we do know a lot of things and we can thank God for them. We can speak truth and pray things like: 'You love celebration, God. You are the one who commanded us to party in the Bible, but we don't know how to right now and we really need some inspiration.' Or: 'Thank you for making our hearts in a way that needs people – it's been so hard without them. I love that you hear us, God, I don't have the words to express the grief, but thank you that you promise to be close to the broken-hearted.'

3 **Invite God to meet you.** We need God's voice, patience, love, truth and guidance. Often our kids fall into a pattern of leaving messages on God's answering machine – they talk at him and then leave. Helping our kids to wait after they've talked to God builds their expectation that God responds to their prayers. Whatever your kid needs from God, encourage them to ask and then to wait 30 seconds, knowing that God moves in response to our prayers. Sometimes we know what God is doing and sometimes we don't, but he *is* doing something – so let's expect him to.

Follow-up

- 'Church – helping kids engage with it' (p. 44) chapter
- parentingforfaith.org/tool/chat-and-catch
- Sessions 4 and 5 of the Parenting for Faith course: **parentingforfaith. org/course**

Next steps

- Are you afraid that your child has been or might be disappointed by God?
- Think about a time when you were disappointed by God. What did you do and what did God do? Is this a story you could share with your child or teen?
- What helps you when you are disappointed by God or struggle to understand what he is doing? How could you create a window into this for your child?

DISENGAGEMENT IN OLDER CHILDREN

RACHEL TURNER S1E70

When our kids are disengaged from God or church, it can feel overwhelming because it's the opposite of our heart for our children. So ask: what are they *actually* disengaged with?

Some of our kids are struggling with God: how do I connect with him? Do I want to connect with him? Does God like me? Is he judging me? That's an unwinding problem – helping kids see and understand God better.

Some of our kids struggle with church. Sometimes they're struggling to go on their own journey while surrounded by people. Sometimes it's monotony – or the sense that nothing in their life 'requires' God.

Depending on what you notice, there are a few different things you can do.

Take a moment to consider what's going on. You could say, 'I'm noticing you're feeling disengaged with this – tell me more. I want to understand, because I've been in that position and so have others. I'd love to hear how you're feeling about church and God in this season.'

It can be helpful to notice what they complain about, what they struggle with or when they shut down. Sometimes you can open a conversation by being honest about your own struggles with church or faith and asking if they've ever felt that too. They can say no, and that's okay – but rather than saying, 'I think you're feeling this', aim for, 'I have felt this – have you ever felt that?' It's about inviting your child into that conversation, because once you know, you can problem solve.

Be proactive. Normalise times in life where we struggle with God or church, so that they don't go, 'Oh no, I'm questioning my faith, I have a doubt, that means I'm not a Christian anymore. Nobody else struggles, so I must be a terrible person. I'm walking away.' It can be helpful for them to know this is something to wade through.

Teenagers often like being provocative and they like debating. It can be helpful to **have conversations where you don't have to know the answers.** Ask them about their friends and experiences; there is so much to crack open and show that this is incredibly relevant to God.

If your kid feels like it's all pointless, grab a book like *Jesus Freaks,* which talks about martyrdom and people who were willing to stand up for their faith to the point of death, or *God is Stranger,* which challenges conventional views of God and gets them thinking. If they find that God has become too 'comfortable', those stories are provocative and bring us aspects of the relevant, purposeful and interesting God.

If your kids are disengaged, sometimes it's because they feel powerless and like God is purposeless. **If you're sensing this in your kid, push into their purpose.** In scripture we find all our heroes have a triangle of identity, relationship and purpose: they know who they are in God, they know how to have a relationship with him and they know what their purpose is. Part two of the book *Parenting Children for a Life of Faith* is entitled 'Parenting children for a life of purpose' and is all about how to help a kid who feels powerless and helpless in the face of society.

Remember, parenting for faith is just about asking, 'What is the next step for my kid and how can I help them take it?' However disengaged they are, there's always a next step.

Follow-up

- 'Church – helping kids engage with it' (p. 44) chapter
- **parentingforfaith.org/post/disengaged-or-disinterested-facebook-live**
- Rachel Turner, *Parenting Children for a Life of Faith: Helping children meet and know God, omnibus edition* (BRF Ministries, 2018)
- D.C. Talk, *Jesus Freaks* (Bethany House, 2005)
- Krish Kandiah, *God is Stranger: What happens when God turns up?* (Hodder and Stoughton, 2018)

Next steps

- If you think your child might be feeling disengaged, spend a bit of time observing them. What do you notice? What do you think might be going on?
- Have there been times when you've felt disengaged from God or church? Why? What happened? How did that change?
- Do you think your child might have a 'comfortable' view of God?

DISENGAGEMENT IN YOUNGER CHILDREN

RACHEL TURNER S1E70

Helping our young children develop a relationship with Jesus can often be fun: enjoying Bible stories together, singing songs, making things. But sometimes what we do just doesn't seem to hold their interest, and it can feel hard to know how to change that.

Let go of the 'shoulds'

Sometimes we feel we're failing. We have these 'shoulds': our kids 'should' be able to listen to the Bible, they 'should' be able to do the Bible craft, they 'should' want to play Bible stories or 'should' engage with Sundays – and these 'shoulds' can trap us into feeling like we need to fix things.

Instead, we can pivot our expectations from 'I expect my kid to engage with all our family faith activities' to:

- I expect God to be talking to my kid, discipling them and engaging them
- I expect that my kid can genuinely love and follow God – I see this in scripture and it's possible for them too
- I expect my kid is having genuine connection with God more than I think
- I expect that I will never see everything happening in my kid's spiritual life

This releases you from a sense of disappointment because you know that God has naturally positioned your kids to meet and know him and it's not something you can force or control.

What are we engaging them in?

Sometimes our faith activities lean towards a child-centric experience, so if our child isn't interested, we stop. But part of discipleship is about creating windows. You can read a children's Bible together and keep connecting with God in that way yourself, even if they wander off. When they see you genuinely connecting with God, even at a young age they realise it's important to you, and you are giving them an insight into your relationship with God.

Sometimes they're disengaged because what you're trying to do doesn't fit their brains. That's okay, it's a hard balance. But when you offer an *invitation* rather than an activity, you're inviting them to do something *with* you so they can flourish like you flourish.

What are we measuring?

We can easily become overly focused on what our children are doing, but it's helpful to pivot from their disengagement with *activities* to the *fruit* shown in their lives. The question is not 'How do I get my kid interested in reading the Bible?' but 'How can I help my kid love God's words?'

Kids may look bored, but three days later they'll say, 'I want to chat to God before bed!' Don't assess the fruit based on what you're seeing in the present, but of what you see over time in their lives.

Look for the micro, not the macro

We often default to looking for the big clear signs that our kid is engaging with spiritual stuff, but miss the tiny moments. Sometimes it might feel like our kids didn't engage at all – but we missed the second where our toddler paused and had a God moment. During prayers in a lockdown Zoom church service, a two-year-old wandered up to a sibling, touched their sore leg, said, 'God' and walked away. Did that child engage with church? No. Did they have a God moment? Yes!

Celebrate your micros rather than your macros – you may be worried that your kid is disengaged in the macros when they have a thousand little micro moments.

Follow-up

* parentingforfaith.org/post/disengaged-or-disinterested-facebook-live

Next steps

* Do you have any 'shoulds' regarding your kid's faith development? Are these helpful for you?
* Can you think of any 'micro' moments where your child has engaged with God – for example, spontaneously singing a song, asking a question about the picture in their story Bible or talking to God?
* How does your child enjoy learning about God or connecting with him? How could you do more of this?

D

DOUBT

JENNIFER FELLOWS, RACHEL TURNER AND KAT WORDSWORTH

The importance of doubt

JENNIFER S2E5

My mum came to faith when I was eight, and she let me in on the journey. We had discussions about faith, the Alpha videos, the questions she had, the doubts she had. She created real windows into her faith, just by us talking about what she was going through. She let me into the doubts and things she struggled with, and that gave me permission to question my faith as I grew up and ultimately to have my own relationship with Jesus.

Doubt is healthy because when children start to doubt, it shows they're thinking about their faith and starting to have ownership over their relationship with God. They're not just following what their family has always done. It's through doubts and questions that we learn to dig deep into God and are able to unwind some of our wrong beliefs about God. We don't need to give our children all the answers; we just need to facilitate them and their own journey of faith and having those questions.

Children's doubt

RACHEL S2E5

Sometimes a child might doubt God's existence because they lack a relationship with him. There's a sense that God may exist, but any kind of connection with him is a challenge. If this is your child, then plugging them into a community of people who are creating windows, framing and unwinding ideas about God when they get stuck – as well as helping your child connect with God in their own way and surfing the waves of their spiritual lives with them – can all help. As they connect with God and see others' experiences, God will become more real.

But a child may also be an 'intellectual wrestler' who needs to understand fully before they believe. So how do we resource children who seek knowledge and need answers to their questions?

1 Let them be them. It's okay to have questions and need to know answers – it's how God has wired them.

2 Don't feel that you need to have all the answers. Your job is to facilitate *them* finding the answers. You are not meant to be the deposit of all knowledge, but to point them to scripture, books, conferences and wise people.

3 Give them places to investigate, learn and argue. Books like *The Case for Christ: Young Readers Edition* or *Is Believing in God Irrational?* are incredible. None of us agree wholeheartedly with any single resource, but part of the joy of having an intellectual wrestler child is saying, 'You won't agree with all this, but it will spark your brain.'

4 Help your kid connect with others like them. Every church has people who have reasoned their way into relationship with God and flourished in that kind of connection. Find them, invite them over, ask them about their journey, have fun with it. You don't have to be a genius, just be you.

When a parent is doubting

KAT S5E4

Part of what contributed to my doubt was having the wrong expectations. I expected God to direct every step of my life, break any fall and always respond clearly. These things aren't necessarily untrue, but we do a disservice to our children when we present them as black-and-white promises, missing out the nuance. I don't want my kids to feel misled or end up with a faith that needs to be totally unpicked when they become adults.

When we read something in the Bible, somewhere else there's often a 'pair'. For example, in Proverbs we read that if you keep God's law, you'll be blessed – but then we read Job and that's not what happens. Humanity is messy. Faith can be hard. Communicating this to children without terrifying or destabilising them is challenging. If you're struggling, pick a story about love. Love is the grounding we all need, and a good starting point.

It can be validating to know that, if you're doubting, you're not alone. Struggling with your faith is common. Seek support – whether you want someone to pick through your questions with you or just someone to take the weight off a bit. We're very good at suffering in silence, but that's not always helpful.

Sometimes if you've got a particular question about something, you can work through it *with* your kids. Find resources and chat to them about it. If you're struggling with prayer, don't just tell your kids it's easy. Talk to them about the reality of it, in an age-appropriate way (that's the difficult part!) and include them in it.

One of the best books we've read is *That's a Good Question!*. My son loves it because it covers questions like 'Were there dinosaurs on the ark?' and 'Will my dog go to heaven?', and I love it because it's instilling in him that it's okay to ask questions, and sometimes the answer is: 'We don't know.' My son isn't fazed by this – kids are more able to deal with doubt than we give them credit for. I want my children to know that no question is too silly or shameful to ask.

Doubt needs to become a more visible conversation in church. It has so much to teach us. I wish it could be a mainstream conversation without stigma. When we open up the conversation, we see that doubt isn't this scary threat to faith, but a catalyst for growth that can be a part of everyone's journey.

Follow-up

- 'Big questions' (p. 35), 'RE lessons' (p. 166) and 'Prayer – struggles and questions' (p. 153) chapters
- Kat Wordsworth, *Let's Talk about Doubt* (Circle Books, 2023)
- Lee Strobel, *The Case for Christ: Young Reader's Edition* (Zonderkidz, 2020)
- Amy Orr-Ewing, *Is Believing in God Irrational?* (IVP, 2008)
- J.John, *That's a Good Question!* (Philo Trust, 2019)
- **parentingforfaith.org/post/intellectual-wrestlers-equipping-kids-who-need-to-know**

Next steps

- What's your experience of doubt? How has it shaped your faith?
- If your child or teen has doubts, do you know what is at the root of them? How could you find out?
- What would you like your child or teen to know about doubt?

EASTER

RACHEL TURNER, ELLE BIRD AND BECKY SEDGWICK

Easter in your family

RACHEL S8E12

It can be stressful thinking, 'How can I communicate the entirety of the salvation message in one weekend?' We get Easter every year, so it's not about trying to embrace the full theological understanding of it but taking a yearly opportunity to delve into a big topic.

Sometimes we prioritise activities over traditions, but traditions are good because they take the thinking out of it. As parents, we can create simple traditions that anchor us, and this will be different for every family. Pick something that your kid is curious about or a truth you want them to grasp.

One family has a special breakfast where everyone contributes. One makes cinnamon rolls, one makes eggs – and they sit around and everybody tells their faith story. Another family does the sunrise service and imagines what it felt like on that first Easter morning. Yet another family reads the sequence of the crucifixion and resurrection gradually, every night, and talks about it. What is a tradition that feels authentic to your family?

Sometimes we don't want our kids to feel the impact of Easter, in case they're worried or sad for Jesus, but it's important and okay for them to feel this. As parents, our job is to help them navigate that. Some kids get into a little shame spiral, but what we get to teach them is that Jesus died so that we could be free from that shame.

In Parenting for Faith, we talk about 'telling the whole story' – the same story, but deeper each time you tell it. I like to use these five anchor points, to shift the focus away from the physicality of the crucifixion and on to the fruit of the Easter story:

1   Jesus came to free us from sin. This isn't something that happened to Jesus – he *chose* to do this for us.

2   Jesus was arrested and put on trial because people were lying about him and trying to trick him. Sometimes people lie about us nowadays, and Jesus knows exactly how that feels.

3   People got scared and left Jesus. Some stood by him. That was a lonely time for Jesus, but he still was loving and kind, saying yes to this process.

4   Jesus died on the cross and took all of our sins.

5   Three days later, he came back to life, which is amazing. The veil in the temple was torn, which means that all of us get to be with God every day of our lives – and that's what Easter is about. I get to talk to God in the shower because of what Jesus did, and I'm so grateful.

Giving kids these anchor points means that as they get older, we can supplement them, telling them more about the arrest and trial, the loneliness, the forgiveness. We can go deeper, but the story will stay the same, rather than constantly revealing new horrors every year.

There are some good Easter resources – but you telling the story the way you know it, and the way you know your kid might need to hear it, can be more powerful. Being able to tell your kid the gospel quickly is a helpful tool.

Willy Wonka and Easter

`ELLE S1E24`

I used the film *Willy Wonka and the Chocolate Factory* to look at Easter as a church family. We talked about this golden ticket being the most amazing thing, giving entrance into the best place ever – and you didn't have to earn it, just find it.

Then at the end of the film, when Charlie thinks all is lost because he's made a mistake, the factory owner sees the good in him and everything changes. All of a sudden, Willy Wonka starts shouting, 'You win, Charlie! You're going to get everything you ever wanted and more!' What Charlie discovers is that this ticket didn't just get him in to see the factory, it was the means by which he inherited everything: the fullness of Willy Wonka's kingdom.

I love that, at Easter, Jesus won the ticket for us. He didn't just get us into a party but into heaven, the place that will be full of joy, peace and our Heavenly Father. We get that full inheritance of heaven because of him. Ephesians 1 says that it's in Jesus that we find out who we are, what we're living for and where we fit in. Long before we first heard of him, he planned us to be part of the overall purpose he is working out.

Jesus' emotions in the Easter story

`BECKY S1E103`

It can be hard for us to see Jesus' humanness, because the gospel stories tell of all the brilliant things he did. We can find ourselves wondering how we can relate to Jesus when we are so very ordinary.

Jesus wasn't superman, he was God – but he chose to put aside all his heavenly superpowers to live as a man. The Bible is clear: he didn't sin, but that doesn't mean he didn't feel the same emotions and struggles as we do.

The stories of Holy Week give us an opportunity to see a side of Jesus that might feel a bit more like us. Using the Parenting for Faith Key Tool of framing, as you're reading the Bible, stop and ask some questions about what Jesus might have been feeling at this point in the story.

For example, in the story of the last supper, you might wonder if Jesus was enjoying the meal with his friends or what he might have felt when he saw Judas leave. When Peter denies Jesus three times, you might ask what Jesus was feeling when he looked at Peter. Or on Palm Sunday: what was Jesus hoping would happen when he rode into Jerusalem? Was he proud? Happy? Fearful? In the garden of Gethsemane when Jesus prayed, what do you think he wanted God to do on the cross? What do you think Jesus was feeling when he looked at his mum?

You might find these questions a springboard into bigger conversations: was it okay for Jesus to feel angry, tired or afraid? Do you ever feel these things? What do you think helped Jesus – could that help you?

Follow-up

- 'Lent and Good Friday' (p. 114) chapter
- parentingforfaith.org/topics/easter

Next steps

- What helps your family have great conversations about Easter? Is there anything in this chapter that prompts new ideas?
- What Easter traditions do you have in your family?
- Do you find Rachel's five anchor points a helpful way to summarise the Easter story? Would you change or add anything?

EATING DISORDERS AND SELF-HARM

DR OLUSEYE ARIKAWE S7E13

Looking for the signs

As parents, we need to be observant. We need to know our children, so that we'll notice when something is wrong. They may become withdrawn or have a sudden change in personality. They may start wearing loose clothing because they don't want you to see their bodies, or become irritable, anxious or depressed. A child with an eating disorder might try to miss mealtimes or avoid eating together, or they might be vomiting, eating more or less than usual, or simply losing weight and you can't explain why. These symptoms can be due to other things, so it's important to seek medical help to find out what's going on.

When parents notice that their child has been self-harming, they are usually distraught and sometimes in shock or disbelief. Young people often don't let their parents know this is happening, because they're worried that their parents are going to be upset. As a doctor, I say to them that it's okay – your parents will worry, but that's their job.

What can we do?

You may want to blame yourself – 'What did I do wrong? Why me? Why my child?'

Stop! As parents, we all try our best, and we're not perfect, but we shouldn't take the blame when our child does things we're not happy with. Often, when a child is struggling, we worry; when we do this, it becomes difficult to support the child. You need to create a safe place for your child and be in a good frame of mind so that you can be there for your child.

Don't freak out. Young people often just want somebody who will listen. They want to feel vulnerable without thinking you're going to judge them. Don't show your alarm at what's happening. Take action, which may include seeking medical or other help, but let them understand that home is a safe place where they can express themselves. Of course you're not happy, but let them understand that you're supportive, you want to find out why, you want to be there for them, you want to see them come out of this difficult time.

So we don't judge, we listen, we get the right specialist help – and, as Christians, we want to pray for and with them.

Help them know God's truth

The important thing is to help them understand who they are in Christ. One major thing that we can teach our children is the love of God. There will be times when your child will doubt that they are really loved by God, so you want your child to know that God loves them no matter what. When they are struggling with self-harm or eating disorders, they have an abnormal perception of their body image. You may see a child who is underweight saying, 'I feel overweight' – so they need to know who they are in Christ.

I love Ephesians 1, which says who we are in Christ: blessed, chosen, adopted, forgiven. No matter how young a child is, let them grow up knowing that God loves them, and whatever they go through, God's love will always be there.

It's important to teach them the word of God, so that when they start to go through difficult times, they will remember these truths.

Often young people going through these things think to themselves, 'God doesn't love me' or 'I'm not worthy of God's love'. Romans 8:1 says there is no condemnation for those who are in Christ Jesus. There's a lot of guilt and condemnation in young people that have eating disorders: they look at themselves in the mirror and don't like what they see. The Bible says, 'Love your neighbour as yourself' (Mark 12:31) so self-love is important, because if you don't love yourself, you can't love your neighbour. If you love yourself, you don't harm yourself. We need to bring understanding that it's biblical to love yourself.

The Bible says you are created in God's image but that's different from what the world says and what our children hear on social media. So our children need to hear the right thing at home. As Christian parents we may understand all this, but children need to know it for themselves; they need to have a personal revelation of this word. No matter how much we pray together and teach them the word, they need to have that personal understanding of it.

When I think of self-harm and destructive behaviours, these Bible verses come to mind:

- 1 Corinthians 6:19–20 – our body is God's temple – God lives inside of us. We don't want to dishonour the temple of God.
- Psalm 139:13–14 – *The Message* reads, 'I thank you, High God – you're breathtaking! Body and soul, I am marvellously made!'

As I've reflected on these, I came up with seven declarations for a young adult who is struggling with body image and whether God loves them. Stand in front of the mirror every morning and just speak these words to yourself – there is power in our declaration. God's word is so full of promises for every issue that we ever go through in life.

They are:

1 I am beauty for my situation (Psalm 139)
2 I am the apple of his eye (Psalm 17:8)
3 I am a masterpiece (Ephesians 2:10) – created in Christ to do good works
4 I am created for God's pleasure (Revelation 4:11)

5 I am God's handiwork (Ephesians 2:10)
6 I am created in God's image (Genesis 1:27)
7 I am created for God's glory (Isaiah 43:7)

Follow-up

- 'Emotions' (p. 82) and 'Illness' (p. 110) chapters
- **wordforher.com**

Next steps

- How might Oluseye's seven declarations be helpful for your kid – no matter what their situation?
- What truths might you want to share with them or remind them of?
- If you are experiencing eating disorders or self-harm in your family, what support do you need for yourself, so that you can continue to support your child?

EMOTIONS

RAE MORFIN, RACHEL TURNER AND LISA CAMPBELL

Struggling with emotional health

RAE S5E6

Emotional health is having a good understanding of the spectrum of our emotions, living equitably with them and understanding that they're all there for a reason. It's about governing them well: not pushing them down, but not letting them take over in decision-making.

We're contending with fear more than ever before, so for our children and young people trying to navigate this scary world, we do them a disservice if we try to smooth out their emotions. When we do that, we're saying that something about them isn't quite right. Emotions are not necessarily neat and tidy, but they're there for a reason. We're all on a journey of learning to navigate them.

Stress is a degree of pressure that we feel which impacts how our brain governs itself. A bit of stress is good for us; it helps us move out of our comfort zones and grow. But the tipping point is when that nervous feeling immobil-ises us. When we can't function or think in the same way, stress becomes unhelpful and unhealthy.

We can't go through life being stressless, so it's about how we turn that stress dial down. Connection combats stress. The Bible talks about perfect love driving out fear. Just coming alongside each other and offering warmth can reduce felt stress.

Jesus was perfect, so in him we see how to govern emotions in a perfect way. He had the full spectrum of emotions – stress in the garden of Gethsemane, anger at the injustice in the temple. He was never out of control; he knew how to channel his emotions. Often he spent time away with the Father – that connection is key.

The Psalms, too, are full of emotions: despair, fear, pouring out our hearts to God. Our connection with God means he can bring his peace and his good-ness, and show us the next step when we're feeling overwhelmed. God is our refuge and firm foundation; he is close and going through it with us.

Helping a neurodivergent child manage emotions with God

RACHEL S1E96

You are the expert in the particular, beautiful way your kid's brain works. Through experience and effort, you know all the little tricks and things that set them off, so you are greatly positioned to help your kid connect with God about their emotions.

Partner with what already works. You already have skills and patterns in place to help your child, so how can you bring in that added layer of faith, God and connection with him? You might set out a visual timetable, saying, 'God, please bring your peace, that we may spend the whole day with calm hearts and joyful faces. Today is not just a series of happenings, but a series of God's peace within those happenings.'

Partner with whatever your child does – but do it outside of the crisis moment. Have conversations about what could be helpful but also what their emotions feel like. Sometimes a child says, 'It feels like fire', or, 'It feels like I'm drowning.' One child said, 'I want a bubble to go around me', and so he would begin to say, 'God, bring your bubble'. He would go into his little space, and it was him and God in the bubble because God knew exactly what he liked and didn't like. Help your child see that God is a God who can connect with them and knows what they need.

Partner with your child's methods of communication with God. We can suggest to our children that it helps manage emotions when we tell God about it. He doesn't need words; he understands and is with you and can help.

Dealing with big emotions

LISA S9E3

Emotions are a beautiful part of how we are fearfully and wonderfully made. They help us work out what's happening around us, keep us safe and enable us to interact with the world. I also think they can be used by God to shape us.

The human brain isn't fully formed at birth and isn't fully matured until you are in your mid- to late-20s. The part most active at birth is the brainstem, responsible for basic functions like breathing, blinking and sucking, but also your fight-flight-freeze response. The thinking part of the brain, known as the prefrontal cortex, is built and continues to develop throughout childhood, adolescence and even through your 20s. When our kids are struggling with big emotions, it's often not about being naughty or making poor choices. Emotional regulation and reasoning are led by the prefrontal cortex, which is incomplete. They don't yet have the ability to emotionally regulate, plan or make good decisions.

Understanding brain development can be very empowering for us as parents. Writing off explosive 'terrible twos' or 'teenage' moments as hormonal can make us feel there's not much we can do, but understanding brain development and knowing that brains are shaped through interaction with safe care-givers, means parents *can* support healthy development.

Emotions that makes us feel unsafe cause our bodies' natural defence system to kick in, switching off the thinking bit of our brain and instead diverting oxygen to other bits of the body we need to help us either fight the danger, run away from it or hide. During those big emotions, our child probably doesn't feel safe. Before we can help them think about why their behaviour was not appropriate, we need their thinking brain to be back online – and we do that by helping them feel safe. In that moment of emotional meltdown, they're in their lower brain, so engage their senses in that space.

One tool is to ask them to say four things they can see, three things they can hear, two things they can smell and one thing they can touch. There are also huge benefits to deep breathing, bringing down your heart rate and signalling safety to your body. So when we're *not* in a meltdown moment, we can teach breathing prayers or hand breathing (tracing around their fingers, taking big breaths in when they go up a finger and out as they go down) – there are loads of suggestions of breathing activities online. This helps their body feel safe and their thinking brain become 'online' again. Then we can discuss why they just kicked their sister or whatever they have done.

We can also help build our children's vocabulary around their emotions by getting into the habit of narrating for them: 'I can see that you're feeling really cross right now because…' or 'I can see that you're really excited about…' Talk through what different feelings look or feel like in their bodies. David does it well in Psalm 39:2–3 – 'But my anguish increased; my heart grew hot within me.'

And this is not just for children – lots of us could benefit from bringing curiosity to our own emotions, becoming conscious of our feelings. When it comes to emotional regulation, looking after ourselves is not something we're always very good at. It's so easy to put everyone else's needs before our own, but investing in our own well-being is important.

Follow-up

- 'Disappointment in God' (p. 61), 'Eating disorders and self-harm' (p. 78) and 'Failure' (p. 87) chapters
- **tlg.org.uk** (Rae Morfin)
- **wonderfulme.org.uk** (Lisa Campbell)

Next steps

- How do you talk about emotions in your family?
- How could you create windows and frame how God helps you deal with big emotions?
- How do you already help your child manage their emotions? Are there any ideas from this chapter you might use?

F

FAILURE

RACHEL TURNER AND KATHARINE HILL

How do we help our kids cope with failure?

RACHEL S1E35

Failure is tough for kids, but we can help our child see it through a different light by celebrating *character* in the journey of failure. Then they learn to see that people's experience is not about whether they succeed or fail, but who they are in the midst of that journey.

There is often so much to admire in what is called a failure: particularly the display of character. If you have kids who are struggling with failure and you want to ground them emotionally and spiritually, watching other people's failures – for example on the sports field – can create interesting opportunities. We can say, 'Failure is a part of life,' and by laying this foundation, you can then talk about it when your kid experiences it. When you're reading scripture you can say, 'When Peter experienced this, on the face of it, *failure* – what was he feeling? I can imagine what that would be like…'

So wade into failure and reflect on character in the midst of people's journeys, to begin to take our kid's eyes off whether it's a success or failure and on to who they are and what they're learning in it.

How do we reconcile God's view of failure with a worldly system that punishes failure?

RACHEL S1E58

Failure is a necessary part of learning and growing. As parents, we can help our children meet with God in the midst of it, getting rid of the shame of not being perfect and embracing the journey of growth with God. But we live in a world that often has competing values. Part of walking with our kids is helping them learn how to navigate life when our values about failure are different.

My suggestions would be:

1 **Frame** for them that other people may think that being imperfect or failing is bad and something to be embarrassed by. Explain that sometimes other people try to make us feel bad or make fun of our mistakes. Tell your kid that you don't expect them to be perfect. You don't expect you to be perfect. You just expect all of us to grow and learn.

2 **Equip** your kid to respond when others try to embarrass them. There was a six-year-old who was very confident that he was a better reader than an eight-year-old, and he would make fun of the eight-year-old for being many reading bands behind him. The parent sat down with the eight-year-old and worked out how he wanted to respond to this: 'That's great you're in gold band. I'm reading better and better every month too.' Phrasing this helped him respond to another kid's different value.

3 Help your kid **see the difference** between being punished for failure and the natural consequences of the learning process. Natural consequences are helpful because they help your kid grow in their confidence to fix their mistakes. Whether it's not finishing schoolwork or kicking the ball in the wrong goal, it's just a natural consequence that they can learn something from. If your kid is constantly being set up for failure – for example, by a teacher, coach or classmate – then as a parent you know you can wade

into that and help fix it. But otherwise it's important that they see you cheering them on in the midst of consequences, rather than feeling it's a punishment that you judge them for.

4 Help your kid **reframe it** for themselves and with God. If their coach or teacher uses a phrase that's against what you believe, help your kid come up with a sentence that changes it. One kid's teacher always said, 'Best foot forward', and that was putting an enormous stress on this child. So the parents sat down with them and brainstormed, and they changed it to, 'Best *try* forward', saying, 'I don't expect you to be perfect all the time but I do expect you to try.'

5 **Train** your kids to take it to God. For example, they could pray, 'My teacher says this – but God, what do you think?' Or, when stressed, to say, 'God, I need your love right now', and breathe deeply for ten seconds and let his peace come, meet with him about it first.

6 **Create windows** into how you cope with failure and mistakes in your life. Tell stories of how God coaches you through it and how you navigate your mistakes, because that lays a foundation.

Failure and emotional well-being

KATHARINE S4E5

Failure is part of life, but there's a silver lining. Psychologists talk about the 'hope circuit' which happens during failure (see *The Hope Circuit*). In Romans 5:3–5, Paul talks about suffering producing perseverance, perseverance producing character, and character producing hope. We don't want to see our children fail, but if we come alongside them, show concern and help them grow through it, we'll be doing them a great service. As our children try again, that hope circuit is created. Layer upon layer, they'll learn to be more resilient, and it will build their emotional well-being.

The definition of resilience is 'bouncing back'; that is, something that's gone out of shape going back to shape again. But recently, experts have been talking about bouncing *forwards* – not just going back to how we were, but learning and growing from a difficult circumstance. We may not want our children to go through challenges, but neural research shows that as our children learn, the connections in their brain grow and they will gradually become more resilient (**drkatetruitt.com**).

Risk-taking is also important. We're hardwired to keep our children safe, but consider how God parents us: he doesn't make our world smaller but allows us to experience new things and learn from them. This is 'anti-fragility' – getting stronger through challenges. We see this in our immune system, our banking system, our bones and, of course, in our children. Help your child to take risks. Give them choices and encourage adventure.

As parents, we want to avoid being both a 'helicopter parent', who swoops in immediately to fix things, and a 'snowplough parent', who makes the road completely flat so there is no risk. There's a lovely proverb: 'Prepare the child for the road, not the road for the child.' It's better that our children learn to take risks when we're there to help than when they're on their own and unprepared.

Experts such as Jennifer Crocker say that one of the most important things for our children's resilience is to give them an awareness of a 'something-bigger-than-me'. For Christian families, we can help our children discover that they are part of God's bigger purpose. The world tells our children to look within to find their identity, but if we can encourage them to look beyond themselves, that's the key building block. As parents, no one knows or loves our child like us; God's placed us to help build that secure identity.

Follow-up

- 'Emotions' (p. 82) chapter
- **parentingforfaith.org/post/how-to-help-them-fail-well-facebook-live**
- Rachel Turner, *Parenting Children for a Life of Faith: Helping children meet and know God, omnibus edition* (BRF Ministries, 2018), ch. 33 'Failure'.
- **careforthefamily.org.uk** (Katharine Hill)
- Katharine Hill, *A Mind of Their Own: Building your child's emotional wellbeing in a post-pandemic world* (Muddy Pearl, 2021)
- Martin Seligman, *The Hope Circuit* (John Murray Press, 2018)
- Dr Kate Truitt, 'Neuroplasticity: The power to overcome and create a resilient brain', **drkatetruitt.com**

Next steps

- What does your child think about failure? How do you know?
- Do you have any stories to share about a time when you're glad you failed because of what you learned from it?
- What is the next step for your child in feeling confident about facing failure?

F

FAITH COMMITMENT

RACHEL TURNER AND CHRISTIE THOMAS

How do I lead my kid to Christ?

RACHEL S1E24 AND S1E51

Please don't feel there's a 'right way' to do this. You're on your journey of walking with God, and you can help your child find theirs.

Very few lifelong commitments happen when you're a kid. Some of us have one big 'becoming a Christian' moment, and some of us don't. Did I understand the full gospel when I made my first commitment to Jesus, aged four? No. Do I now? No. I'm on a constant journey of responding to the gospel over and over again until I see him face to face.

Most often what happens is kids are exposed to the gospel and want to respond. For some, that turns into their big moment of commitment with God, and for others it's small connections with him that lay foundations.

Instead of thinking, 'How can I help my kid have their "big moment"?', I find it helpful to think, 'How do I help my kid respond to the gospel to the best of their ability?' Romans 10:9 says: 'Declare with your mouth, "Jesus is Lord", and believe in your heart that God raised him from the dead.' This looks different for every kid and every season they're in, so my suggestion is that you help them know how to respond to the gospel every time they feel prompted. How?

1 Show your journey of faith. **Create windows** not only into the story of your big commitment, but also into how you live life responding to the gospel again and again. Tell stories of your lifetime of responding to the gospel, of when you realised this and when you responded to that, and what God did.

2 Equip your kid to know *how* to respond, rather than feeling like you need to lead them through their experience. You could say, 'If you ever want to tell God what you believe about him, God wants to hear all of it.' Empowering them to do it on their own enables them to constantly respond to all of the messages of the gospel.

So be encouraged, there's not one thing to get right or wrong; it's about weaving a whole path for our kids to constantly respond to the gospel that they know.

Making a faith commitment

CHRISTIE S7E1

Many kids growing up in church don't have a conversion-moment memory. For most, it just happens in these small daily moments, especially if they're growing up with Christian parents talking to them. I use my phone's notes app to write these down, because I don't want to forget.

When my kids were five and almost three, I overheard the little one saying, 'I have Jesus in my heart.' The five-year-old said, 'No you don't, *I have Jesus in my* heart!', to which the little one said, 'Yes, I *do* have Jesus in my heart!'

Then the older one said, 'No you don't, you have to ask him: "Jesus will you please come into my brother's heart? Thank you, Amen."' I came out of the bathroom and said, 'What were you talking about?' They wouldn't tell me, so I asked the little one, 'Have you got Jesus in your heart?' and he said, 'Yes!'

I have no idea what brought on that conversation, but I'm convinced God was moving. God did it, not me – I wasn't even in the room! I know God sees those moments and honours them. Even if my kids don't remember, those are the things that keep turning their faces back to God.

The process of God turning our hearts to him looks a bit different in each person's life. I chose to get baptised around 14, but others need to be asked by their parents. 'Do you think this is the time for you?' We don't want to push our kids into something they're not ready for, but sometimes we need to ask, 'Are you serious about this?' Sometimes it's just fear holding us back from making those professions.

In terms of readiness, I would look for a child who seems to be earnestly loving God – not a child who isn't making mistakes or has an adult faith, but a child who cares about what God thinks. They'll probably have done some version of a sinner's prayer, understand the gospel and how it impacts their life. Every child is different, and you know your child.

Is my child ready for a public faith declaration?

RACHEL S1E74

Although it's the parent/carer's role to help a child come to this decision, often we can feel like we're helpless until the church brings it up. But you can feel powerful to have these conversations with your child.

A few considerations:

1 Know your church's policy. Do they have specific age markers? Talk to your church leadership and find out what's available and when, so it's in mind before you have to decide.

2 Create a framework before you get there. Start talking about it. **Create windows** by taking your kids to a confirmation/baptism/communion. Watch it and **frame** it, talking them through what people are doing, why they think someone would choose this and the difference it makes in their life.

3 Help them know what the next step is, so that it's not just dependent on a church announcement, but your child feeling powerful to take the next step. Regularly talk about the next step, encouraging them to talk to you when they're ready to find out more.

4 Have your own sense of what you want to see. You know your kid and what they need spiritually. Some of us will say yes immediately, and some of us will want to investigate and get our kid on a course. It's up to you, but it's helpful to think ahead of time what you are looking for in your child. Trust your parental instinct and value each kid as their own person on their own spiritual journey.

Follow-up

- parentingforfaith.org/post/summary-sin-forgiveness-and-salvation
- littleshootsdeeproots.com (Christie Thomas)

Next steps

- What was your journey of becoming a Christian – was there one big moment or lots of little moments? Could you share that with your child?
- How does your child respond to the gospel they know? What might their next step be?
- If your child is older, can you remember the times they responded to the gospel when they were younger?

F

FRIENDSHIP DRAMAS

OLLY GOLDENBERG, RACHEL TURNER AND CLARE LUTHER

Navigating friendship difficulties

OLLY S4E3

If your child is having difficulties with a friend, that friend might be going through a troubled time, so ask, 'What do you think they need from you at this time?' Or, if it's becoming a pattern, 'We've noticed they keep treating you this way – is that a good friendship?'

It's helpful to communicate what friendship looks like. An unhealthy friendship is where one is putting down the other, not allowing them to be themselves and is very focused on the needs of one individual. A healthy friendship is where everyone is built up, free to be themselves. Additionally, some friends help our children coast, while others stretch them to be the better version of themselves.

When our children struggle with friendships, point them to the friend who will never let them down: Jesus. When our kids go to the Lord as their stable friend, he may point out to them the need to say sorry or be more friendly, lovingly opening things up in a way we couldn't as parents.

Often, we're willing to pray for our children to make the right friends, because of a fear of making the wrong friendships. But what if we were to switch our prayer of fear into a prayer of faith? For example: 'Lord, I believe you're sending them to this school for a reason. You know who you want them to connect with; let those connections be made where they'll be influenced for good but also where they will be a good influence on others.'

We're called to love everybody, but not necessarily to be everybody's friend. Encouraging our children to live in a way that is good, kind and looking out for those in need is all part of a journey with Jesus. Who's not being loved at the moment? Is it that child who's sitting by themself? I'll go and sit with them. Does that mean I'm becoming their friend? Maybe, maybe not. It's freeing for kids when we say that we're not asking them to be everyone's friend but just to notice when somebody needs a little bit of companionship. Friendship means opening ourselves up in a way that means we could be hurt. You must love others – but you don't have to be friends with them.

When kids are being mean

RACHEL S1E8

If another child is being mean to them, children can feel powerless. When we equip them to cope with the meanness, they feel proactive and not helpless. Here are four ideas for equipping them:

1 **Encourage our kids for true confidence.** Other children might pick away at our children's confidence, but as parents we can build in our children a confidence that's not based on what they're good at but on what they bring to their community.

2 **Frame it well.** You could say: 'When people are angry, it's usually because they're experiencing emotions and aren't coping very well. They want to feel powerful and don't know how, so they make other people feel small. This isn't okay, but it's what you're seeing.'

3 **Give techniques.** Sometimes our kids need permission to walk away, or to practise one or two sentences that they could say, as well as how to connect to God in the middle of it.

4 **Create windows.** There are mean people in every life circumstance, so telling stories of what we struggle with, what yweou're trying and how we feel about it, is crucial for our kids in seeing that this is something they will encounter again, but God is helping us and can help them too.

Making new friends in a new place

RACHEL S3E6

When you move to a new place, often you gravitate towards the people who are easiest to be around. But sometimes our kids need permission to move on from the friends they started with. When they realise they've reached the limit of how much they can trust their new 'friends', it's time to go choose the friends they actually want to be with. Real friendships are when you get to know someone more and choose to let them into your heart.

It doesn't mean they have to walk away and break up, but start looking around for the kind of friend they would want to have in the closer part of their life. We can encourage them to be brave and start conversations with people who are kind, as well as sometimes being the person who sucks up others who need someone.

Sometimes talking about the 'wrong crowd' can be unhelpful. It's more about using your wisdom to decide who you trust, who brings you joy and who would produce the fruit in your heart that you want. When you're joining a new place, you just want people to hang out with, so talk about the difference between these people and true friends.

Managing emotions around friendships

Prayer is the best starting point. Because we come into parenting with a 'packed suitcase' of our own experiences, we can set up anxiety without even realising it. So, we need Jesus to help us understand ourselves and our children: 'Where am I at, and what are my worries for my child? Have I started talking in a way that indicates that friendships might be difficult for them?'

When someone's being unkind to our child, the worldly default is to put ourselves first. But people are unkind when they're hurting. So instead of storming into school to complain, the first port of call is to say to our child, 'I can see that wasn't a nice experience for you. Let's talk to Jesus about your feelings and pray for that person. Let's pray we can be different with them. We don't have to be best friends, but we can love them in the way Jesus shows us.' That's the joy of seeing God work through the way we speak to our children.

Be present and consistent. If friendships aren't happening for your child, give them time to chat through their emotions when they come home. Don't try to fix it. If we're getting in a panic, they're going to pick up on that. It is so important to model to our children the need to depend on Christ, in a way that is calm, allowing them to experience emotions and come out the other side. I encourage parents to live by five pillars: compassion, connection, co-regulation, context and conversation. If we can put those into our everyday communication with our kids, we're already winning; they need to feel seen, heard and validated. If we can make home as safe as possible for them, then we are doing a brilliant job. They will grow in a groundedness that the world can't explain. It's painful – I'm not denying that – but be patient.

I have an 'A&E' framework of emotional well-being – applying just one of the following can make a significant difference:

- **Assumptions and expectations** – if you're freaking out at your child's big emotions, pray for a clear head and calm tongue. Your child needs to know they are being heard, without judgement, so allow their emotions to surface.
- **Acknowledge and explore** – use their words and ask open-ended questions to explore what happened.

- **Address and explain** – be kind and use literal language to give context to what they've experienced.
- **Be available and encourage** your child – be present to listen. Pray.
- **Apply with examples** – chat through a time when you felt like they are feeling, to model and normalise. Empathise.

Follow-up

- parentingforfaith.org/post/summary-friendships
- childrencan.co.uk (Olly Goldenberg)
- clareluther.co.uk

Next steps

- What are your children's current experiences of friendship?
- How do you respond when another child is unkind to your child?
- What stories do you have of friendship difficulties – can you use them to create a window into how God helps you?

G

GAMING

BEN JONES S1E116

Children spend a huge amount of time gaming. We should ask:

- Are our children playing in isolation? If so, do we know what or who they're engaging with and how they're interacting with people?
- What are the opportunities for us to use games to lead to conversation?

Games can unpack conversations about life, personal, local and global concerns, emotional well-being, adventure and competition. But to do this, we need to explore and understand how our child is interacting with the game:

- **Narrative** – what narrative are they hearing? What are they gauging from this game?
- **Experience** – what are they seeing?
- **Emotion** – how does this game make them feel?

From those, we can begin to ask:

- Is this healthy for you?
- Are you feeling uncomfortable about this?

It's tempting to think kids are safe because they're at home, but they can hear unkind, hurtful comments through online gaming. Isolation doesn't help, which is why it's good to work out how you can explore these games together.

Understanding a game's narrative and why our child wants to be part of that is important for us as parents, so that when they ask to play a particular game, we can say, 'So you're okay with the idea of fighting zombies/shooting people/blowing things up?' or whatever the game entails. When you start to understand the context of the game, you can ask your child to self-reflect, leading to a conversation about whether to play the game. If there's a TV series alongside (e.g. one of the Marvel shows), watching that together can help understand the narrative of the game, so that a child doesn't feel left out but can decide when they want to play it. We're giving them ownership.

A game like Minecraft offers great opportunities to reflect. Your child might build something that articulates an issue they're facing. The object or context allows them to discuss the issue openly, without it becoming a threat or an uncomfortable conversation. They might then say, 'I feel *this* about *that...*' It can also be a great opportunity to explore and discuss Bible stories, giving your child the chance to reflect.

Follow-up

- 'Pornography' (p. 138) and 'Social media' (p. 194) chapters
- parentingforfaith.org/post/summary-gaming
- missionalgen.co.uk (Ben Jones)

Next steps

- What's your family's approach to and experience of gaming?
- Do you have fears around your children's gaming? What opportunities might there be?
- What's your next step with regards to gaming? What's your child's?

G

GRACE

MELISSA KRUGER AND RACHEL TURNER

His grace is enough

MELISSA S3E9

Children are aware when they've done wrong things, so to start with this place of us *both* needing grace makes it an even playing field. I've been alive longer, so I've sinned more – I'm the bigger needer of grace – but kids carry shame and that's why they hide what they've done. I want to turn the script and say confession, not hiding, is the way to freedom.

Everyone's going to make mistakes, because we are products of the fall. What do we do with the sin problem? You may try to fix it by doing everything right: mowing the lawn, getting good grades in school, cleaning the whole house – but you don't get God's grace by trying really hard. Lots of kids live in fear of doing anything wrong; it's a good thing to want to do what's right, but if everyone's going to struggle with sin, then these kids need the answer too.

It doesn't matter what we've done, God's grace is big enough. One day our kids will commit a sin they think is too big for God's grace – we all have – so they need a reminder that his grace is enough.

To a young child, I would describe mercy as being released from what you deserve (i.e. a punishment), but grace as getting good things when you deserve bad things. In some sense we were total enemies of God, and now we're made sons and daughters. We are invited to his table to feast with the king. Grace is totally a gift. You didn't do anything to earn it. In fact, what you earned was something bad – and what you got was something good.

As parents, we need to remember we need grace too. We can get frustrated with our children, thinking, 'How have they not learned this by now?' But I'm struck by the parable of the unmerciful servant (Matthew 18). Jesus paints this picture of someone who's been given great mercy, yet is unwilling to be merciful – and sometimes, as parents, we can be like the unmerciful servant to our children. Even though we're still struggling with sin and have been forgiven this big debt, we expect our children to have learned obedience in ways that maybe we aren't even obeying yet. If we understood the grace that has been given to us, we would be more patient in dealing with our child's need of the same grace. Grace changes everything about how we parent, because if I view myself as a fellow sinner in need of grace, my invitation to my child is going to be so different. Rather than frustration and impatience, it's going to be one of love, kindness and gentleness because I just want to invite them to Jesus.

To see a parent say 'I'm sorry' is such a powerful learning tool, because our kids will one day have to apologise to their children, their spouse and their friends. We're teaching them what life in the fallen world looks like. It's important, though, that kids understand what makes that 'sorry' okay. 'Sorry' isn't the magic word – it only works because grace has been given in Christ. I want them to understand that on the cross Jesus was paying our debt.

Helping younger kids understand grace

RACHEL S1E19

At around seven to eight years old, kids' brains change. Before that age, they understand concrete concepts, but they struggle with metaphors and abstract thought. Young children can understand that they have sin and need to get rid of it to get into heaven, but the idea that God has given us grace through Jesus, so it's not all on us, is a complex thought that they will still be grasping. It's okay for them to be in the middle and not have a complete understanding. Trust that as you are communicating and shaping this concept for them, they will go deeper the older they get, because you're modelling the same thing.

To help them grasp this abstract concept, find a moment in your everyday life when you can give them an experience of grace. Take a time when they do something wrong, explain that they messed up and what the consequence of their actions would usually be – but explain that today you're going to show them grace. You're going to give up your screentime instead of them giving up theirs, because the consequence still needs to be paid but you're going to do it for them. That's grace – you don't deserve it but I'm going to give it up instead of you, so that we can stay connected.

Create windows into how grace works for you: 'I want to please God and I know I fail. I'm so grateful that my failure doesn't mean I'm going to be separated from God forever, because Jesus makes up the difference.' Giving your child an experience of grace may begin to help, but also remember that their brain will develop into it.

Follow-up

- 'Shame' (p. 183) and 'Sin' (p. 189) chapters
- Melissa Kruger, *His Grace is Enough: How God makes it right when we've got it wrong* (The Good Book Company, 2022)

Next steps

- Does your child understand what grace is? How could you help them understand it?
- How could you create windows into the grace you've experienced from God and the difference it made?
- How might seeing yourself as 'a fellow sinner in need of grace' influence your parenting?

H

HALLOWEEN

RACHEL TURNER
(S1E119 AND HALLOWEEN BONUS EPISODE IN SEASON 1)

Making your mind up about Halloween

Throughout life, our kids will face an enormous number of scenarios where they have to decide who they are as Christians, how the world impacts them, what their faith is and how that faith informs those decisions. Halloween is an opportunity to coach our kids through being in the world but not of the world.

Here are three steps to navigate it.

In our church communities, there are many different views about Halloween. Some people see it as an amazing outreach opportunity, while others feel like engaging with it is to engage with something evil. So, firstly, wherever you are on this scale – even if you feel like you know what you think – examine it, because knowing your reasons is important.

In Romans 14, Paul talks about 'disputable matters', and verse 12 says that each of us will give an account of ourselves to God. Therefore, it is our job as Christian parents to work out what we believe, how our family is going to engage with it, and why. Often, we arrive at a decision but can't quite say the 'why'. Is it because of scripture? Is it because of what God's saying to you when you pray about it? Is it because of the community that you live in and the values that you have? Establish the 'why', so that when you say, 'This is what we've decided', it's not just because it's what you've always done, but because of your specific kids and context.

Secondly, find a comfortable way to explain your choice to your children and equip them to embrace that value too. Often, we just give them the answer – but teaching them how to engage with a world that isn't God-centred is a useful skill. A younger child in nursery might be offered scary colouring pictures, so equip them to say, 'Excuse me, I don't like this picture. Can I please have another one?' If we don't equip our kids to engage with it, they'll feel powerless, and we never want them to feel that, particularly when dealing with a conflict between the world and God.

For tweens and teens, explain how your beliefs impact your choices and how going against what you feel is right impacts your connection with God, because they need to see the effect of violating the decisions you've made for yourself. Ask open-ended questions to hear their views. When they don't agree with you, it's not a conflict; it's them being willing to explain their thought process to you. Let them talk. Teenagers will make mistakes because they're learning to own their choices – so help them debrief, letting them change their mind without saying 'I told you so'. We are positioned to journey alongside our teenagers as they decide how to engage with the world.

Finally, don't judge others for their choice. In Romans 14, Paul asks who are we to judge one another? Other Christian families are just like us, trying to figure it out and being accountable to God for their choices. We want to be a supportive community who defends each other even if we don't agree, because we know we share the same goal of pleasing God. Pay attention to who God is shaping your family to be and accept others who have made different choices. In doing so, we teach our kids to honour others in their decision.

Finding your family's fit at Halloween

When making decisions around Halloween, firstly find out yourself what is being proposed – whether an activity, film or event – that your child wants to engage with. Often things come through somebody else's filter, but if you're going to decide what's right for your kid, then it's got to come through your filter because you're the one God put in the life of your kid.

Secondly, consider what is spiritually healthy for your kid, rather than the 'right answer'. 1 Corinthians 10:23 says everything is permissible but not everything is beneficial. Assessing whether things are objectively good or bad is difficult, so ask instead how it is *beneficial* or *constructive* to the spiritual health of your child. That may be different from other people's kids. Your job isn't to decide what's right for everybody, but what's right for your kid.

Thirdly, be confident in a community of faith. We want to create a parenting community of people who want the best spiritual health for each other's children – people who bless you, listen to you, encourage you and help you, and for whom you can do likewise.

Why do people like being scared?

How do we explain to our children why people want to celebrate Halloween?

Here's my explanation. (You don't have to agree!)

> People who aren't sure about God don't know that they can be full of love, peace, kindness and power in this life. They don't know the truth about who God is, what he does and all the realms that we can't see. All they know is that there's darkness around that is scary, uncontrollable and beyond what they know. So if they make fun of it and try to create scenarios where they're in charge of that scariness (by making haunted houses or watching scary movies or whatever), it makes them laugh and they can feel powerful and not out of control.

> It's a trick to make what is scary fun – but I don't need to do that. I'm not scared by ghosts or demons because I know that God is bigger and more powerful. I know what we have is better and deeper than all of that. I don't celebrate it because I want what is more fun and joyful than what that stuff could ever be.

Then you can have a good conversation about what's next. Are you scared by those things? Why? Who is God in this? You can create windows into how you cope when you're scared, and help your children learn to do that too.

Follow-up

- 'Supernatural' (p. 202) chapter
- **parentingforfaith.org/topics/halloween**

Next steps

- What do you think about Halloween? How could you explain your position to your children in a way that helps them understand why you've reached that decision?
- How do you think your family might approach Halloween this year?
- Does your child find Halloween scary? Do you find Rachel's explanation helpful?

I

ILLNESS

RACHEL TURNER, JESSIKA SANDERS AND
ERIC M. SCHUMACHER

Illness of a parent

RACHEL S5E7

My kid was six when we found out I had cancer.

The only thing I could offer him was who God was in this. There were so many things I didn't know and couldn't tell him – like if my journey would end in death or disability – but I could put his feet on the one who doesn't change.

I explained what was happening to my body and how that was different from what happens in the spiritual. I said, 'There's a poison in my body called cancer. We don't know how strong it is, so we're going to investigate it and get treatment. Sometimes it ends badly and sometimes great, but what's more important is that God's with us through it all. I'm going to look for who God is because he's not going to change, no matter what.'

I knew this was a journey of many conversations and constant discipleship of how to connect with God. It became about watching my kid and thinking what I could frame for him. One bedtime, for example, we were talking about fear. We sat there and sang 'No longer slaves' four or five times in a row. It was a wonderful time of worshipping in the moment. Bedtimes became a time to share what God had been teaching us that day – endless opportunities to ask, 'How are you feeling about this?'

It's easy to beat yourself up about your own faith journey through illness, but there's no wrong way of experiencing what you're experiencing. A helpful switch for me was, 'How do I help *my kid* through what they're going through?' rather than what I'm going through. I'm wondering if I'm going to die, but he's experiencing an exhausted parent in pain. My job is to help him meet with God about *his* experience, not mine – so even when I wasn't able to figure out where I was positioning myself, I could still help him take his next step in faith.

In terms of support, the thing I wanted most was for everyone to stay normal. I didn't want my world to change or for cancer to be the biggest thing in my life, so I valued people's willingness to talk about themselves and their stress. If I only had a limited amount of time in this life, I wanted to be a good friend.

Practically, I loved it when people took everyday stuff off me so that I had the energy to be the parent I wanted to be. Kind people picked up my kid from school so I had the energy when he got home to give him a hug and ask about his day. They'd take him to his after-school club so I could nap. If you're supporting someone going through illness, rather than saying, 'What can I do?', say, 'I want you to have the energy to do what you want to do with your kids, so what stuff can I take off you?' When people brought food, they asked for my recipes so they could cook what was normal for my family, and I didn't feel like I was failing them. That was so powerful for me.

Helping kids process the illness of a sibling

ERIC AND JESSIKA S10E3

Eric: You're the expert on your child. You know best what to share with them, so use your discernment. Acknowledge that something significant is happening, give them freedom to ask questions and don't be afraid to share your own sorrow because that helps them know it's okay to be sad or fearful. Then go to Jesus with them, reminding them that even if we don't understand and can't control what's happening, we have a Saviour who loves us, died for us, rose for us and is redeeming all things. We can trust him in the middle of illness.

Jessika: Help your kids to process and name their feelings. My kids really enjoyed breath prayers: breathe in for three seconds, hold for two and exhale for five. But also pair that with scripture, to calm their hearts and minds.

Video calls were such a gift for us because my children didn't get to meet their sibling until he was one month old. Talking on the phone and praying together was another way to stay connected. It communicated that, though mum and dad are far away, we can still connect with them; it just looks a bit different right now.

Eric: If you're home with your kids, to whatever extent possible, maintain some sort of structure in their life – do fun things with them, do normal things, give them a sense of stability. Although this crisis is taking centre stage right now, it's not the whole of life. We can stay in the word with them, maybe reading through a gospel where we see Jesus controlling all sorts of situations. Eliza Huie's *Count Yourself Calm* is a good resource for taking big feelings to a big God. The 'Inside Out' movies talk about the importance of not ignoring your feelings, but not letting them control you. As we develop that language with our kids of identifying their feelings, we can pair those emotions with gospel truths. The child might be angry, fearful or sad. Help them to name that, then share what the hope of Jesus says to those feelings and pray with them.

Jessika: Chris Morphew's *Why Does God Let Bad Things Happen?* is good for those over nine years old. God doesn't promise a life without trouble, but he does promise that he's going to work things for good. Our testimony is so important. What you're walking through right now won't be wasted; you have no idea how God will use that for his glory.

One thing I share with my children is the idea of Immanuel – God with us. In moments of desperation and hard times, you can visualise God in the room. What does that look like? I can imagine him holding you, catching your tears, wiping them away. Visualising can be powerful and comforting.

Eric: Jesus suffered and went through crisis. In the garden of Gethsemane, he said, 'My soul is overwhelmed with sorrow to the point of death' (Matthew 26:38). On the cross, he's asked, 'My God, my God, why have you forsaken me?' (Matthew 27:46). Jesus had these experiences like our children do. When they're asking questions or don't feel they can face tomorrow, they don't have to be ashamed, and Jesus isn't ashamed of them. He entered that experience, died on the cross for our sins and rose from the dead so that he would be able to help us in our time of need. He is for us.

Follow-up

- 'Death and bereavement' (p. 53) and 'Death of a child or parent' (p. 57) chapters
- Jessika Sanders and Eric M. Schumacher, *In His Hands: Prayers for your child or baby in a medical crisis* (The Good Book Company, 2024)
- Eliza Huie, *Count Yourself Calm: Taking BIG feelings to a BIG God* (The Good Book Company, 2023)
- Chris Morphew, *Why Does God Let Bad Things Happen?* (The Good Book Company, 2021)
- **parentingforfaith.org/post/grateful-for-cancer**

Next steps

- What emotions do your children have around illness? How can you help them name and share them?
- How could you create a window into or frame who God has been for you in times of family illness?
- If your kids are experiencing a close family member's illness, how could you encourage them to connect with God about this situation and how they are feeling?

LENT AND GOOD FRIDAY

RACHEL TURNER S1E23

Framing Lent

As parents, we get to help our kids develop a balanced view of God and unwind wrong views of him. The information and experiences that our kids pick up form a lens through which they see God. It's our job to help make that lens as accurate as possible.

If we're not careful, the concept of giving up something for Lent can easily, within a child's mind, be warped into the idea that God is about you having a joyless life. We know that's not true, but if we are going to expose them to 40 days of people giving up stuff, it's important to coach them through what that means, because fasting is a key part of our faith, through which we can understand God's heart.

If you don't follow Lent traditions, that doesn't mean you miss the opportunity to help steward your kids' views. You can frame for them what's going on – not just what fasting is and where it's found in the Bible, but the 'why' behind it. There are so many questions our kids have:

- Why are we fasting?
- Why does giving up something random help us draw closer to God?
- Why do we do it for 40 days as opposed to one day?
- Why would God ask us to do that?
- Why does fasting make us focus on God more?

If we answer the 'why', we give our kids an understanding of the process of transformation we're on and how our choices affect our relationship with God. If we only focus on the 'what', we give our kids only an understanding of the *behaviour* of religion rather than the *heart* of the relationship.

If you fast for Lent, explain why you've chosen what you've chosen and what you're hoping is going to happen in your relationship with God. What has he been doing, and what are your reflections on that transformation process? If you've given up your fast after a few days, the journey of success, failure, self-control and what God's asked us to do is so valuable for your kid to see.

So whatever your journey of Lent, explain the 'why', because it unwinds the view of God being a stringent task master who wants to suck joy out of life. He is a God who takes us on journeys of experimentation to show us something new of his heart and ours, that we may be more connected.

Sin and Good Friday

Sometimes we over-focus on the mechanisms of crucifixion and how painful it was – but that can disconnect kids, because we're essentially saying, 'Look at the horrible thing you did to Jesus.'

Rather than speaking of blame, it's more useful to talk to children about sin – not, 'Sin hurts God – look how painful it is', but, 'Why was the cross necessary?' and 'What does that mean today, for me?'

In everyday life, there's a clear process for sin: you make a mistake, there's a consequence and usually an apology. We'll often use the same idea spiritu-ally: you made a mistake, so say sorry to Jesus, then we can move on. But sin is more than this. Sin is something that clogs our hearts and makes us run away from God, forming a blockage and weighing us down.

We can tell kids that before Jesus came, we were trapped and isolated from God. Sin is the choices that break God's laws of love and the clean heart he calls us to. Ask: what does it feel like when you know you've made a bad choice? That feeling is our awareness of our sin, our unclean heart. And what does God do in response to that?

Share your stories. How do you know you need to ask God's forgiveness? How do you know when you've made a bad choice? Create a window into your life, helping your kids understand that however disconnected we feel, Jesus came to wipe that away, so that we may be ever connected to God. Then, when we think about the cross, we're seeing him provide a way for us when we've messed up. He is inviting us out of the corner and into relationship with God.

It's also important to help kids identify the difference between shame and conviction. Beating ourselves up about sin, hiding from God or saying mean things over ourselves is shame. Even when kids have restored relationships and come to God, they might cling on to disconnection, and that's not what God has for them. Paul says, 'All have sinned and fall short of the glory of God' (Romans 3:23), and 'What I want to do I do not do, but what I hate I do' (Romans 7:15), expressing this constant frustration and understanding that we're on a journey, trying to live out the freedom Jesus has purchased for us. We're going to make mistakes, but that doesn't mean we live disconnected from God, and we are so grateful for that.

As you do Good Friday, don't focus on 'We are terrible sinners', but be in awe that this is the day that changed how we live forever – and that is exciting.

Follow-up

- 'Easter' (p. 74) chapter
- parentingforfaith.org/post/good-friday-for-under-5s
- parentingforfaith.org/tool/unwinding

Next steps

- If you give up something at Lent, do your kids know why you do it or how you hope it will bring you close to God? How could you help them understand the 'why' of what you do?
- How do your children understand sin?
- What windows could you create into your life with God that will help your kids see how you know when you need forgiveness?

L

LYING

RACHEL TURNER S1E48

Lying is often connected to children growing an understanding of how people work, how to get what they want and a desire to hide mistakes because of a fear of punishment. Most children go through this 'figuring out' phase, but every child's personality is different: some don't struggle and others do. But if your child is developing a habitual pattern of deceitfulness, it can feel awful. Here are my thoughts – but remember you know your kid best and so you'll know what will work. God wants us to cast off sin so that we can be in relationship with him. Think about how you can set your kid up for success, and remove any hindrances. Then make the conversation about relationship, rather than what not to do.

Firstly, remove hindrances. Some things we do as parents to problem-solve behaviour can end up reinforcing it. We all do this accidentally sometimes – a lot of parenting is about noticing when our 'solutions' are becoming motivators in our children's behaviour and fixing it. For example, bribing our children into good behaviour may cause them to lie to continue to get those rewards.

Looking at how we respond when our children mess up can help fix some of the reasons behind why they're being deceitful. This isn't the whole reason, but it can be a factor.

Secondly, shift the conversation to be about relationship. Say: 'I want our relationship to be so good that there's nothing you feel you can't tell me, even when you make bad choices. It's my job to help and encourage you as you work out the consequences of those – and when you fix those messes, I'm proud of you. If I catch you lying, then that dishonesty builds a wall between us. It puts us on separate sides. That's why there are consequences to lying, because lies hurt relationships, and I don't want that to be a pattern in your friendships or your marriage or in your relationships with us.' When we frame it as a hurt relationship, we can talk about consequences, but also that honesty draws us closer together.

Thirdly, talk about trust. Help your child understand that trusting them to be honest leads to greater freedom and bigger choices, but if they can't be trusted then we must use our parent powers to make choices for them. When they do something obediently, say: 'Thank you for being faithful and building my trust in you.' Building trust is powerful; it means that when your child asks for something, you can model how the trust they've built up impacts your response. This also happens when they mess up and tell you. You can say: 'I'm sad you made those choices, but I'm also so proud of you for telling me. That builds my trust that you're going to fix your mistakes.'

Follow-up

- 'Failure' (p. 87), 'Grace' (p. 103), 'Shame' (p. 183) and 'Sin' (p. 189) chapters

Next steps

- Is there anything in your relationship with your child that might accidentally be encouraging them to lie?
- Do you think your child is confident they could talk to you about a wrong choice that they have made?
- Children don't always realise adults face the same temptations about truth as they do. Could you share a story about a time when you were tempted to lie? What happened? Where was God in it?

M

MONEY

JESS MONTEIRO S4E4

Laying good foundations

I'm a huge advocate for having honest conversations with our children about money. Our kids see us pay for things with our phones – which eradicates an understanding of the value of money. So be intentional in teaching children that we go to work and get paid for our time, and that looks like money. Look at physical money. You could make a game out of it: looking at what £10 used to buy us and what it buys us now – ensuring that children gain a solid understanding of what money is. If your children can grasp that, then you can start conversations about your own family's finances – but otherwise I would protect them from it. During these foundational years, we don't want to impart anything that may make our children feel fearful, when we're there to protect them.

We can also give security to our children in the way they observe our life: how we behave, our financial disciplines, our restraint. We want them to see our priorities and generosity, not our panic-buying or irrational spending. In times of fear about money, speak truth over your household. Be intentional about praying together, starting with what you're thankful for. You're establishing a foundational understanding that even when mum and dad can't provide, God will.

Generosity

Settle on your message about those who are socially excluded, because we might say one thing yet do another. We know God calls us to be generous, but do we believe it? Or are we thinking, 'They should be claiming benefits/ They're claiming too many benefits/They could have a house if they wanted'? Because then we're stuck: we want our kids to be generous, believing that the world of the generous gets larger and larger, but are adding this caveat: 'They're probably not using it for what you think they should use it for.' If we can shake off the caveat, then our kids will see our generosity a lot more authentically and regularly because we're just doing what God calls us to do, and God will deal with the rest.

There also needs to be a fundamental understanding of sacrifice – not, 'If you give that, we won't have it, so we're not going to give', but, 'Are we in agreement as a family that if we give this, we won't have it?' That is gold to teach our kids. If they choose generosity, we're stoked; if they choose to keep it, we're stoked, because they understand its value.

Trust your kids. They will often be more creative than us in ways to love, because they're not bound by context or expectations. Listen to how they want to help, because it might be the best idea, something we can action, and that's super helpful for their growth. Follow their lead to love like they love, because they'll love hard.

It can be hard to know why God doesn't just 'fix' all the financial difficulty in the world, particularly when it's our family who is struggling. I would suggest it's about understanding that God uses people to partner with him, to be part of the change. We are the answer, we are the church, and he is changing people's situations through us, giving a way forward for so many. We can explain to our kids that we don't have the answer to why everything isn't fixed, but we have deep joy in walking with God daily while he uses us to bring about change. Living authentically connected into his call and that nudge of the Holy Spirit means we will see God move. Then our conversations at the end of the day don't look like, 'Why does God not fix it all?', because they see God fixing it piece by piece, person by person.

Sometimes we can hide behind the question of why God doesn't just click a magic button and fix everything, but God has called us very clearly to love the poor, so that must be the best answer. We must lean into the teachings of Jesus about feeding, clothing, including and loving – then our kids will see the most incredible moves of God, and grow up speaking of his generosity.

Money worries

As Christians, we believe in a God who provides for us. We are not anxious about anything, but with everything we're prayerful. So if you're struggling with money, seek help – your child will see the way you're dealing with your situation. So many times at CAP (Christians Against Poverty), we see situations that could have been easily handled earlier on, but are in a much worse state simply because people wanted to hide it. Trust that God hears the cries of your heart. Give CAP a ring, we can help – your situation doesn't need to stay the same.

In times of financial difficulty, I believe we are called to be calm, focused on Jesus and not afraid. Our kids need to see the strength of God and the certainty that we will continue to be generous – and we will see the fullness of God as he gives us our daily bread. Not always getting their 'wants' may be tough for kids, but what we can establish in them is a faith in God that will see them through lack or plenty for the rest of their life. Let's raise children who not only understand budgeting, but how to replace fear with peace, what their 'lack' is and what they have in Christ. Nothing will ever replace the truth of the Bible and the fact that we are not called to be in panic but of sound mind, at peace with what has been and what will come.

Follow-up

- capuk.org
- parentingforfaith.org/post/talking-to-kids-about-money

Next steps

- How do you talk about money in your family? Do your children grasp what money is and how it works?
- How could you use the idea of sacrifice to teach the sort of generosity God has shown us and wants us to show others?
- How could you create windows into your own relationship with money? If you are financially comfortable now, could you share stories of times when you needed to lean into God and others and what happened?

M

MOVING

DAN HAWKEN, STEPHANIE FOSTER AND JO AND ELLIOTT IRETON

Transitions

DAN S10E6

As a family, we felt God calling us to move out of our town and for me to move into church work. We talked with a church and started to make plans: go for the job, put the house on the market and move in the summer, so our boys could start school in September. But in April some odd things started to happen to me physically. I couldn't walk in a straight line, I became clumsy, I developed a stutter, and I started getting involuntary movements in my left arm and torso. I was referred to neurology and, besides lots of tests, they said I couldn't drive, which meant I couldn't commute to my current job or take on the new one.

We didn't know what to do; the plan wasn't working out – but we still felt it was the right thing. So we waited. In August, I was allowed to drive again and diagnosed with functional neurological disorder. We were back on track with our plan, just a little late. I went for the interview, got the job and we put the house on the market. I would start the new job in November, we'd stay temporarily with my parents, then move around Christmas, so the boys would be home-schooled for two months. However, God had different ideas! In December the house sale fell through. In February we got back on track with a new plan to move at Easter – but again our house purchase fell through in March. We decided to put the boys into school at Easter, which meant we had to commute them every day. Finally, in September – about ten months after we'd relocated – we moved into our house.

In one sense we were fortunate that my condition was physical: our kids could clearly see that Daddy wasn't right. We would say, 'We don't know what's going on, but we do know the person who does know – and that's God.' We spent a lot of time in prayer with them, and explaining that we're scared as well, but we know God's in control and that his plans are best. The eldest was very interested and wanted to know everything, whereas the younger two didn't necessarily want to know everything, so we didn't burden them with too much information that they didn't understand.

We hadn't said much to them about moving house, because we knew it was going to be delayed, but moving in temporarily with my parents was helpful for them because they knew my parents' house. They were sad about leaving school and friends, so we tried to focus on things that weren't changing, such as family, grandparents and toys!

Home-schooling gave us opportunities to do new things. My parents live in the Forest of Dean, so we were able to go out and learn a lot more about nature and trees. One of the boys picked up a Roman book and got excited about Rome; there's some local baths near us, so we went and explored them.

During times of change, emotions run high for both parents and children. We found it helpful to talk about them and name them. Are we scared? Are we upset? What are we upset about? Children pick up on a lot, so it's good to be honest with them, helping them understand that it's okay for them to be scared and unsure, but then taking it to the next step of prayer. We had several plans – but God had a better one.

Moving abroad

STEPHANIE S9E10

Two years ago, God started to highlight Dubai to us.

Life was good. We enjoyed our jobs and felt settled, but it became apparent that God was asking us to move. Processes that should have taken months took days. Eventually, we'd packed and were waiting for God to tell us to go. The day before we left, I had a dream which was clear: move! Then my husband received some prophetic words. We booked our tickets, and the next day we were on a flight.

Some of our friends were worried for us, but we said, 'No, you don't have to be. The onus is on God.' We've gone through all the emotions, but God has been so faithful: every single day we hear from him. I used to pray, 'God, what is your purpose for my life?' because I didn't want a 9–5. Our strength and comfort come from knowing that this is where God wants us.

God prepared our kids for the move too. Even before we told them about it, they watched a YouTube programme where a family went to Dubai – and started talking about wanting to go there! When we eventually told them about the move, their devotional that day was about moving (Ruth and Naomi) and they were excited. Once the plane landed, the questions started: 'When are we going back? When are we going to see our cousins?' Our role has been about reminding them that we've moved now; this is where we are. Family will come and visit, and we will also go and visit. God was gracious in how he prepped them and aligned it all.

I won't say we've settled in fully; it's been a slower process than we'd hoped and we're still transitioning. There is a new culture and religion. My daughter is learning about prayer mats and the Quran. I want her to be confident in her faith, but also to be aware and tolerant of different faiths. This journey has brought us closer together as a family. God made it clear that this journey would be for the five of us, saying, 'Don't worry about the kids, I'm helping them, I'm journeying with them.' It's been great to talk about Jesus, learn scriptures and just become more immersed in our faith together.

Communication and transparency are so important. As parents, sometimes we want to shield our kids from things we're going through. We're wondering how to explain it or worried they might not understand. But these kids are their own person. We might take the primary decision, but we need to communicate well and carry them along with us. Any questions, we can talk them through and frame why we are making the decision we're making. We can be open about not being sure what lies ahead, because our anchor is Jesus. We're trusting God, who won't let our feet slip (Psalm 121:3). Sometimes your kids might be more understanding or even encourage you on this journey.

Keep God at the centre. Pray through your kids' worries. Maybe they're worried they won't find friends, but God orders your steps – so believe that wherever you're going, God has a community there for you.

Moving multiple times

JO AND ELLIOTT S1E19

As a child, I (Elliot) moved around a lot. My Christian parents were very good at talking to us about possible moves, involving us in praying about where God wanted us to be. We wanted to do the same with our kids, so we've always tried to have open and honest conversations about potential moves, with frequent dialogue, prayer and worship.

Our biggest move – from north London to Kenya – was a very long process of prayer and discernment. When it started to feel like God was moving us on, before we knew the destination, we involved the kids, asking them where they thought God wanted us to be and what he wanted us to be doing. It was such a big move that it wasn't enough for the two of us to be praying and listening – we wanted the kids to do the same. It was about worshipping and waiting on God together, but also having a conversation with them, asking them what they thought God was saying. We wanted to have assurance that it wasn't just 'God said to us', but 'God spoke to our family'. Once you've moved, you can look back and see where God was speaking and guiding.

Sometimes God gives a prophetic word or picture with interpretation. Other times we've heard God speak through wise things our kids say – for example, 'Wherever we go, we know God's with us.' If we've been given a prompt from God, it's not necessarily about where we're going; sometimes it's a reminder of who God is. His faithfulness becomes part of the rudder for directing our family.

Looking at my own childhood, there were moves that, as siblings, we had different views about – yet my parents moved anyway. They had to trust that, even if there was anxiety, God was leading. As parents, sometimes we have to make difficult decisions. If our kids were to have concerns or questions, it would all go into the melting pot – that's discernment. It's important to value our kids' thoughts, views and feelings equally as our own. Ultimately, we will make the decision, but it's important that they're involved in that.

It's never a case of 'Daddy/Mummy is moving jobs therefore we're going here'; it's always been in the context of being called *as a whole family*. We're all going to start this new adventure, wherever that might be. Moving hasn't always been easy, but journeying together as a family means God becomes your anchor. You know that God has asked us to do this, to be here and we're responding to that call as a family.

When we moved to our current parish, we came to visit as a family. Going to bed that night, we asked, 'What do you feel about the place?', and they said, 'We have to move there!' You realise that God is using the enthusiasm they've caught for this place to speak to us. We might not know how things are going to work out, but the kids' excitement for the move will help carry us through anxieties and challenges that will undoubtedly come up. That excitement is useful in making the first step to move.

Follow-up

- parentingforfaith.org/topics/transitions
- Rachel Turner, *Comfort in Uncertain Times: Helping children draw close to God through biblical stories of anxiety, loss and transition* (BRF Ministries, 2022)

Next steps

- If you are facing a move, how can you show your kids the part God is playing in your move and/or your decision-making?
- As well as talking as a family, how can you encourage your kids to chat to God about the changes and their feelings, and catch what he says back?
- How could you create a window into how God is helping you or has helped you adapt to a new situation?

N

NEW SIBLINGS

ANNA HAWKEN AND LUCY RYCROFT

Gaining a sibling

ANNA S7E11

As we always say at Parenting for Faith, there's no one right way to do things – you're the expert in your own kids.

We've prepared for a new sibling differently at different stages, depending on our kids' personalities and ages. Most recently, for our older children, it's been about giving them responsibility, but also letting them be kids, whereas with my youngest it's been more about explanations. She's not been through this before, so we're trying to help her understand what's going to happen, where she fits, where mummy and daddy are and where God is.

A framework for helping them see where God fits in has been:

- **Connecting your child to you** – making time, stopping the important thing you're trying to do to listen to their question, talking with them, sharing news or helping them be part of a process.

- **Connecting your child to God** – involving them in praying for their new sibling, chatting and catching about their feelings, facilitating their own relationship with God without being like the high priest. Part of stretching yourself between more children is that it helpfully stops you being that 'middle man' all the time, because you'll sometimes be with another child: 'I'm here to support you, to give ideas, to equip you – but more and more you can take ownership.'

- **Giving your child next steps to connect with God** – for a toddler: 'I'm leaving you in your bed now, but you and God can keep chatting about the new baby'. With older ones, it might be giving them Bible notes or tools to help them with a passage.

How can I apply the Parenting for Faith Key Tools? In any situation, I think: 'What are the Key Tools and how can I apply them?'

Framing:
- Books – explaining life with a new sibling, how a baby is made, etc.
- Apps – to share the baby's growth, week by week
- Invite questions – welcome and validate all feelings
- (In the context of recurrent miscarriage) Explain the complexity, complications and risks of growing a human

Chat and catch prompts, to encourage your child to connect with God:
- Tell God how you're feeling about your new sibling
- Tell God anything you're worried about
- Ask God what kind of sister/brother he wants you to be
- Ask God what he loves about your new sister/brother

Adoption

LUCY S7EP11

When we were first thinking about adoption, my daughter would often ask, 'Are you going to have another baby?' So we used those opportunities to say, 'We think God might be asking us to parent a child whose tummy mummy [birth mother] can't keep them safe and warm.'

When we started the process, it was about involving our kids as much as possible, because most of our social worker meetings happened when they were at school, so they weren't really part of what was going on. My husband and I went to the adoption panel during the school day, but when they came home we shared the good news and went out for a celebratory tea together.

Closer to our boys' arrival, the older two chose gifts for their new brothers and got involved in preparing their bedroom. We bought photo toys for our new boys, where we could pop in photos of the four of us and record our voices saying, for example, 'Hello, I'm... and I'm your new sister', and we sent these to the boys' foster home.

In terms of preparing our community, I was conscious that adoption can be a taboo subject. I didn't want everybody else on the school playground whispering about our family. I was perhaps a bit hyper-sensitive, but we were still new to the school. I didn't want to make life difficult for our children.

So I did a few things:

- Prepared the school community by going into my son's class to share about adoption and answer questions
- Prepared our friends by creating a book for their children with photos and simple words to explain our adoption journey
- Prepared our parents and siblings by giving them the book *Related by Adoption*
- Our parents went on a 'Related by Adoption' course run by the local authority

Asking for help

Anna: One of the most powerful things we can do is to say 'yes' to everyone who offers to help. The classic thing people say is 'Let me know if you need anything.' That's really hard! But if you've got a meal rota to give them or a list of jobs, that's much easier. Be specific. Let God guide you in that. I find it tricky to ask for help, but when I'm honest with God, he's quite good at nudging me and sending someone – then I have to say yes!

Lucy: You could also set up a WhatsApp support group and ask those 'some-ones' if they'd like to be part of it. Then when you're sending out a request, it doesn't feel as hard because you're not directing it at one person. I'm a bit of a wuss when it comes to asking for help, but I don't mind asking a group because I know that individuals aren't then feeling like it's all on them.

My top tip is to be open with people, answer questions and invite honesty, because the worst thing you can do is hide away. A few years down the line, when you might be struggling more, it's easy to become isolated. We need to do what we can to keep people around us.

Soon after our boys came home, a school mum asked, 'Are they going to call you Mum?' After all I'd been through to adopt my boys, and all I would go through for them, the idea they wouldn't call me Mum could have been quite offensive! But taking offence doesn't do anyone any favours. I just had to answer that question openly, because the fact other people come to you and ask is a great thing. Don't berate somebody for their lack of education; use their questions to be part of that education.

Follow-up

- 'Sibling rivalry' (p. 186) chapter
- parentingforfaith.org/post/the-bedtime-routine-what-is-important – the framework Anna mentioned comes from here
- Hedi Argent, *Related by Adoption: A handbook for grandparents and other relatives* (BAAF, 2011)
- thehopefilledfamily.com (Lucy Rycroft)

Next steps

- If you are helping your children prepare for a new sibling, which of these ideas stood out for you?
- God's given us a church community to surround and support us and our children. What might that look like for your family if you are expecting a new sibling – or what might that look like for you if you are part of a church supporting a family?
- How could you use the framework of connecting your child to you and God and giving them next steps to help your children with other tricky or new situations?

P

PARTNERS WHO ARE IN A DIFFERENT PLACE ON THEIR FAITH JOURNEY

RUTH MORGANS AND CATHY BOND

Discipling together

RUTH S5EP8

Everyone's relationship with God is individual – and that's true even in a relationship where your partner does have a strong relationship with God. Their relationship with God is theirs, and yours is yours. My husband is a bit further along his faith journey than when we first met, but he's still exploring what it looks like to have his own personal relationship with God. It's been something we've navigated together within parenting.

When I first got married and we had children, I thought that my role in discipling them was to create activity-based ideas, so we'd do devotionals or a little Bible study and it did feel like something I was doing on my own. But Parenting for Faith has allowed my husband to be involved more rather than less with the children's discipleship, because we recognise that their faith is their own. I don't have to step in and pray for them or teach them what the Bible is saying; I just ask questions that help them connect to God – and my husband is more than capable of asking those open-ended questions too. 'What did you think about that? Where did you see God in this story?' Wherever he is on his journey, he can partake in that. So where before it was about coming to sit at the table with mummy, now it's conversations over the table that the whole family joins in with.

I'm not saying that we're not still intentional within our family of how we disciple our children – there certainly are some things that we plan out – but I feel like Parenting for Faith has introduced a way that my husband can be involved in discipleship in an equal way to me too, because I'm not responsible for my children's relationship with God, nor is my husband. We're just responsible for creating a space where we talk about spirituality. I found that very releasing.

There's a bit on the six-stage circle (**parentingforfaith.org/post/the-six-stage-circle**) that talks about establishing boundaries. When you're in a relationship with somebody, they are involved in creating boundaries for your family, and that doesn't only have to be boundaries around mealtimes or going out or money, but also around the expectations of faith, whether you're on a similar point in your faith journey or a different point. When we had children, my husband and I created some boundaries together around what faith would look like, because it's such a big part of my life and because he's open to it being a part of our family life. So, for example, he does come to church because it's very difficult for me to work for church and look after our children. He comes to help the children, and that was a boundary that we agreed on together. However, he doesn't want to spend his whole summer holiday at Christian festivals, so that's a boundary he put in. Whatever position you're in, if you have a discussion about boundaries and set them together, then you're all involved in the circle of discipleship, wherever you are.

We're all changing

CATHY S5E8

I used to worry that my husband's faith journey was not progressing, but the more I pray about this and listen to him and journey with him, the more I realise that there is a progression. He is super-supportive of everything the children and I do within the church, but I never want to force anything on him. Any deep conversations come from friends that he has through church.

I sometimes look at families where both parents are Christians, going to church every week, on their faith journeys – and I see perfection. I have to remind myself that, no, we've all got imperfections. I've had moments where I've thought, 'Life would be easier if…' – but again, no, God's put me in this position, on this journey with my amazing husband.

My eldest child is 32 and my youngest is 15, so we've been on a long parenting journey. I've got a jar called 'Family question time', but rather than having all faith-based questions, I've got a mix, from 'What's your favourite movie?' to 'Where did you feel God was in your day today?', and the whole family gets to answer. Over the years we've had different answers as the children have matured and changed and as I and my husband have, and it's been interesting to be able to do it together.

The fact that my husband is on his own faith journey, just at a different stage, has always encouraged me. At church, I've learned to not say I'm on my own, because in parenting I'm not on my own: I have the support of my husband. I'm so much more understanding of the fact that God puts us in relationship not just with him but with our family, and I have every confidence that he is walking with me while I walk with my family members, no matter where they are on their faith journey. I used to feel sad if I didn't get invited to something because it was couples, or sad if I was invited to things and I was there on my own, but now I don't feel like that. My faith journey has grown and matured, and I feel so much more relaxed in these situations. And the more relaxed I've become, the more my husband attends church things.

Follow-up

- parentingforfaith.org/post/the-six-stage-circle

Next steps

- If your partner is at a different place on their faith journey to you, what in this chapter resonates with you?
- How could you encourage conversations about faith that the whole family can join in with?
- What boundaries do you and your partner have around what faith in your family looks like?

PORNOGRAPHY

IAN HENDERSON S7E10

Pornography has been around for a long time: even Ancient Greek pots have naked pictures. Today, it's an old enemy using new weapons – and with the rise of broadband and smartphones, it has completely shifted. Porn is now more accessible, anonymous, addictive and affordable than it's ever been – because this is the first generation with anytime-anywhere access to this unregulated content.

More accessible

In 2021, just one porn site received 54 billion hits – 150 million a day. In context, recent football tournaments have been getting 50–60 million live views. When I was a teenager, a shopkeeper would check my age. Online, young people don't have to prove their age. There's a box you tick saying you are over 18 – it's even easier than setting up a Snapchat account.

More dangerous

Porn used to be just naked pictures in magazines. But now if you put 'porn' into Google, the first search results are usually aggressive, violent and 'hard-core' content.

In January 2023 the Children's Commissioner published a report around porn use among children and young people. She mentions a girl who disclosed her first kiss. The boy she was kissing (aged twelve) strangled her, saying he did that because he saw it in porn and thought that was normal. We hear stories like that all the time through our schools work. Around 88% of the 100 most-viewed porn videos show aggression towards women, and that is starting to shape what young people consider normal.

More affordable

The porn site mentioned above is a free site. There used to be a pay barrier to buying pornographic magazines or videos, but now it's free – you just have to watch adverts.

The Children's Commissioner report stated the average age of a child's first exposure to pornography as 13. By age 9, 10% had seen pornography; this went up to 27% by age 11. This isn't a problem just for adults. We can't ask our parents, 'How did you do it with me?', because this is a new landscape, so we've got to find new ways of navigating that with our children.

Framing the dangers of pornography for children

There are lots of positives about the technological advance we've seen over the last decade, and it's important as parents that we don't just wrap our kids in cotton wool and keep them away from any tech.

The internet is like a city: a great place with loads of entertainment, education, culture and community, but it also has dodgy places and dangerous people. We have to teach our kids to figure out what's good and avoid what's dangerous. When my kids were six years old, there's no way I would jump in the car, drive to the city centre and say, 'I've got housework to do, why don't you jump out and wander around' – I would never dream of it! But we often say, 'I'm busy, just go on this phone that hasn't got any parental controls.'

We need to use the skills we would use in the city and apply them to the internet. We might have to educate ourselves and then put in some filters. When kids are younger, there are more controls, more 'hand holding' – perhaps by not having a browser on your child's phone straight away or setting it up so they have to ask permission for new apps. As they get older, that changes; it becomes more about conversations than controls.

What to do when your child is exposed to porn

If your child is exposed to pornography, chances are it's not because they went looking for it, so teach them that if they ever see something upsetting, they should follow the 'three Ts':

- Turn it off
- Turn away
- Tell me

Assure your child that this is not something you get in trouble for: 'I want us to be able to talk about this, to make sure we can keep you safe, but you will not be in trouble. You don't need to keep this a secret.'

I'd recommend the books *Good Pictures, Bad Pictures* (aimed at 7–12s) and *Chicken Clicking* (aimed at 3–7s). The latter talks a bit more generically about online safety.

I'd also recommend **internetmatters.org**, which has been set up for parents by internet service providers. It contains advice on what apps are out there (and the pros and cons), tutorials on how to set up parental controls on different devices and how you put restrictions on YouTube.

If you're struggling with porn

Naked Truth was set up to open eyes and free lives from the damaging impact of porn. Half of our work is educational, helping people navigate this issue. The other side is supporting those who are either struggling themselves, or maybe for a spouse/partner wanting help for themselves because there's been betrayal and hurt.

We run online programmes, groups and counselling so anyone can access them. A lot of our amazing team have their own story too, so they come with training and expertise but also with empathy. There's no shame or judgement. It's been amazing to see hundreds of people who perhaps have given up hope: as they've been intentional, doing scary things like asking for help and joining some groups, they have found change.

We have so many people who are saying that, after decades of feeling like porn was controlling them, they're now free from it. So it is possible for porn not to be in your future – whether as a user or partner.

Follow-up

- 'Social media' (p. 194) chapter
- parentingforfaith.org/topics/relationships-gender-and-sexuality
- Dame Rachel de Souza, '"A lot of it is actually just abuse": Young people and pornography', 31 January 2023, **childrenscommissioner.gov. uk/resource/a-lot-of-it-is-actually-just-abuse-young-people-and-pornography**
- **nakedtruthproject.com** – for educational resources and help with beating porn addiction
- Kristen A. Jenson, *Good Pictures Bad Pictures: Porn-proofing today's young kids* (Glen Cove Press, 2019)
- Jeanne Willis, *Chicken Clicking* (Andersen Press, 2015)
- **internetmatters.org**

Next steps

- Do you know if your kid has seen or accesses pornography? How could you open up a conversation with them – what 'curious questions' could you use (**parentingforfaith.org/post/curious-questions**)?
- How could you equip your child to know what to do if they come across pornography or something that upsets them? Do you think the 'three Ts' would be useful?
- Share a story with your kid about a time you made a wrong or damaging choice. What did you do? What did God do?

P

PRAYER

RACHEL TURNER, MATT VARAH WILSON AND HELENA WHITWELL

Different types of prayer

RACHEL S1E56

Chat and catch is us stepping *out* of our children's connection with God. We help them create space to be honest with God, coaching them on how to recognise God's communications.

Intercession is bringing something to God, 'standing in the gap' and asking God to act. We can model this by interceding for our children; they love hearing what we say to God about them. We can also give them opportunities to 'stand in the gap' for us and others.

Corporate prayer is a group of people getting together to pray. Sometimes, with children and young people, this feels like pulling teeth because they're not yet comfortable in having a one-to-one conversation with God, so it feels more awkward to talk to him in front of others. If your kids are more reticent in corporate prayer, that's okay – they're still growing. But describe to them what's happening: people coming together with the same heart around a topic. Make it normal for your kids, reassuring them that it's tricky to know what to say sometimes, but that their words help others express their hearts to God. It's okay to say something little – their voice is important. It's also helpful for kids to know how to engage with others' prayers – that when they agree, they can say 'Amen'.

Help your kids identify these different heart positions so that they learn to be comfortable engaging with their Father God in different ways. A life of prayer is a wonderful thing, and you can help them in all of it.

A theology of prayer

RACHEL S1E69

When we talk about prayer, our first stop is often the Lord's Prayer, a simple, vulnerable expression to God as a loving, involved Father, with no pressure to say the right things or look fancy.

But this isn't the only time we learn about conversational prayer in scripture:

- **Exodus 33:11** – God's relationship with Moses is described as 'face to face, as one speaks to a friend'. Enabling our children to grow close to God is incredibly significant – it doesn't diminish God or make our children respect him less. Moses was never in danger of thinking that God wasn't holy or powerful. He had this face-to-face with God and was in deep awe of him. What a gift for our kids to know that the God who is so awesome also cares about them and wants friendship with them.

- **Psalm 6:3** – the Psalms are full of people chatting to God in open, messy expressions. This one says, 'My soul is in deep anguish.' They're sometimes beautiful, sometimes an awkward cacophony of people wholeheartedly expressing despair: a no-holds-barred open communication with God. Our kids can tell God everything, uncensored, with no performance. God isn't waiting for the right prayer formula; he wants to hear it all.

- **The gospels** – every time someone talked to Jesus, they were technically praying. From the disciples discussing who would be greater in the kingdom, to laughing and chatting on the road, to deep questioning and confusion, it was all life with God. Our kids need this 'all day, every day' access to God woven into the boring bits of life. If they feel confident to share half a thought with God as well as long, involved conversations, they'll have the gift the disciples had.

Jesus said not to 'keep on babbling like pagans' (Matthew 6:7) and some think that means we shouldn't use a lot of words. But Jesus said this so we'd know that prayer isn't about charming God with fancy words or looking impressive to others. Getting kids to pray isn't about them praying aloud so we can hear but giving them the gift of their own personal connection with God. Then corporate prayer becomes an expression of what's already inside them, rather than their first step in praying.

Asking God for what we need

MATT S6E6

As parents, we're used to being asked for everything. A lot of the time we try to do everything in our own strength – and the things we can't do, we'll annoy God about! But how can we ask him for more things continually? The three scriptures that I've always leaned on are:

- **Job 42:2 'I know that you can do all things'** – kids often expect us to know all things when we don't – but God does. This gives us a good picture of who he is.

- **Jeremiah 32:27 'I am the Lord, the God of all mankind. Is anything too hard for me?'** – again, this gives us a better picture of who we're speaking to. If God made the highest heavens, the earth, the sea and everything in them, is anything too hard for him?

- **Job 36:7 'He does not take his eyes off the righteous'** – we're righteous because of Jesus, so God never withdraws his eyes from us. He is always there, taking care of us, whether we sense him or not. We're not called to be feelers, we're called to be believers. God is also the only Father that's never been broken – he's literally perfect in love.

As parents, we can only do so much for our kids, but we can steer them to the place where they get the other stuff from God. One summer, we didn't have much money. We were on our way to a wedding and our car broke down. The next day, as we walked to church, my daughter and I started to pray for a car, knowing we didn't have the money to buy a new one. Within 30 minutes of praying, a guy came up to us at church and gave us his car keys. He said, 'This morning at 6.00 am, God told me to give you my car.' He didn't even know what had happened. So we drove our new car back from church! This guy then didn't have a car, so I had to pick him up for two weeks, which was a bit awkward. But two weeks later an older guy came to church. He didn't know anything about what had happened, but gave the man who gave us his car an envelope containing a cheque for four times what the car he'd given us was worth! We had come to the end of our resources as parents, so the kids got to see the heavenly Father's resources at play.

A key verse for us is: 'Do not be anxious about anything, but in every situation, by prayer and petition, with thanksgiving, present your requests to God' (Philippians 4:6). We don't get everything we pray for, but our kids have seen many big answers to prayer, and it's so key that they get their own testimonies, rather than just hearing about our testimony. The more you get kids involved in prayer, the more they're going to see results from prayer – and that's going to cause their life with God to go to another level.

Giving feedback

RACHEL S1E18

As parents, we often try to get our kids to pray, but training them on what happens when they pray and how it impacts others is a significant part of equipping them for a life of prayer.

We love it when kids pray for us, but the danger is that our response can be patronising. They're not praying to be cute, so when we respond in that way, it robs them of seeing the power of their prayer. We want our kids to know that when they pray, God hears and responds. Here are my three tips:

1 **Create opportunities for them to pray.** When opportunities come up where being prayed for would be helpful, your kids may jump in or may need to be asked. But inviting them to pray for you is a significant way of communicating that you expect God to move when they pray.

2 **Prepare to receive from God.** No matter how small your kid is or how new they are to prayer, they're praying so that God will do something in your life. We can grow in our expectation that God is listening to these tiny prayers and will move. When we do, it says so much to our kids about what we believe about God, them and prayer.

3 **Feedback afterwards.** Whatever God did while your kid prayed for you – whether you felt more peaceful or whatever – give feedback. But don't make things up! You can say, 'I'm not sure what God did, but I absolutely know that he did something', to lay that foundational belief that when they pray, God does something. Then feed back to them later, at dinner time or breakfast the next morning or two weeks on: 'Hey, remember when you prayed for me? This is the story of what happened next in my life. Thank you for doing that.'

Guided prayer in pregnancy

HELENA S1E92

I was blessed with positive birth experiences, and enjoyed bringing God into it. I loved to speak his truth over the pregnancy and birth, declare his goodness and know that I could trust him.

I noticed it was common to experience fear and trauma through pregnancy and birth, so after I had my children, I became passionate about others having positive experiences. As Christians, we believe in the power of the almighty God. That doesn't mean things will always go to plan, but knowing God's with us through every circumstance makes a massive difference.

I got together four church friends who were all pregnant with their first child, to pray for each other, their babies and their upcoming births. We listened to each other for what God might be saying to them and their babies and it was powerful. These days I run regular events online.

Pregnancy prayer is about finding ways to connect with God, asking him how he's feeling about the baby he is creating inside of you and his plans for them. But it's also important to focus on you and your journey of becoming a mother. In pregnancy, we'll often have anxieties about things, but there are so many scriptures about trusting God and casting our burdens on him.

It's also helpful to be specific in prayer. In my pregnancy, I thought about my ideal birth and I wanted to do it with God, so I prayed that my labour would start at 9.00 am in the morning after a really good night's sleep. Some people might think it's silly or unrealistic to pray something specific like that – but I can testify that my first labour started at 9.00 am after an amazing night's sleep! There were other things that didn't work out like that, but that was one that did happen.

Follow-up

- 'Prayer – chat and catch' (p. 148) and 'Prayer – struggles and questions' (p. 153) chapters
- **parentingforfaith.org/topics/prayer**
- **prayerstorm.org** (Matt Varah Wilson)
- **christianbirthsupport.co.uk** (Helena Whitwell)

Next steps

- What is your experience of prayer?
- What would you like your child to understand about prayer? How could you widen their experience of prayer?
- Share some stories of times you've prayed and what God has done.

P

PRAYER
CHAT AND CATCH

RACHEL TURNER, ANNA HAWKEN AND KIRSTY WILMOTT

The high priest

RACHEL, S1E78

A long time ago, people connected to God via a high priest. Because of Jesus' death and resurrection, we no longer need anyone between us and God, but have full access to God and can pray directly to him. I think sometimes, as parents, through great intentions of wanting to facilitate God-connection, we accidentally stand in that role as high priest. Instead, we can reposition ourselves to 'coach' our kids to find their own path with God while giving boundaries and safety.

Getting started with chat and catch

ANNA S2E3

'Chatting' is just encouraging children to use informal language or to draw or to make something to communicate with God. We use 'catching' instead of 'listening' because God communicates in many ways – a feeling, a thought, a Bible verse, something God plants in their mind, a voice – however God chooses to communicate. We want children to be ready to 'catch' from God, just like they get ready to catch a ball.

How do you get started with this? Model chat and catch in big things and little things – you might need to do that out loud. Explore with your child the ways people hear God's voice – it's rarely as an audible voice. And experiment – ask God a question, and see if you catch an answer.

Praying with under-fives

ANNA S1E20

What does prayer look like for little people?

Firstly, they don't have to do it in their heads. For a small person, that's often tricky. When you give them a prompt to chat to God about something, they will almost certainly shout it out loud. That's not a problem, but just keep directing the conversation back to God. For three- or four-year-olds, you can encourage them to whisper their answer into their hand or a pillow, hide under their covers, whisper to the wall – whatever works for them.

Secondly, it doesn't have to be verbal. Kids can draw pictures or make something out of playdough. God is a proud parent who wants to see their new skills. They can show God that they've just learnt to clap their hands or how fast they can zoom on their scooter.

Thirdly, weave conversational prayer into whatever you're already doing. For under-fives, so much of their life is playing, so they can chat to God about what they're doing with their toys. Focus on the things that interest them and that they can see. If you're walking to playgroup with a child in the buggy, you might want to point out the flowers and ask them to tell God which one they like best. If they're watching TV, they can tell God which character they'd most like to be or what's making them laugh. It doesn't have to be about things that are traditionally 'spiritual' – it can be about whatever they're into.

Finally, use their emotions as prompts. If something great happens – maybe they peed on the potty – great! Let's tell God about that! Maybe they're excited about a new toy, so let's show God what it can do. But it's also about the sad, difficult times: maybe their friend snatched their toy – tell God how that makes them feel; they fell over and bumped their knee – let's show God where it hurts, and ask him to make it better.

Emotional intelligence

RACHEL S1E8

One of the things that can get in the way of our children's chatting and catching with God is limited emotional vocabulary. If they only know 'happy' and 'sad', they will struggle to articulate all the stuff in the middle.

So we can facilitate *extra-verbal* communication. I tell kids sometimes that if they don't know what word to use, just make the noise – like 'Urgh! God I'm feeling urgh!' or just cry to God.

But we can also teach our kids more emotion words. Ashamed, embarrassed, misunderstood, peaceful, excited, regretful, betrayed, joyful, nervous, worried, proud, grateful, lonely, content, scared and relieved are all good emotion words to learn to identify. David and the other psalmists are all over the place emotionally, talking about vengeance, fear, desperation and hope. So when your kid is experiencing an emotion, help them learn to identify it by saying, 'You look sad, but do you think maybe you're feeling regret, like you wish that hadn't happened?'

Create windows into your own emotions. You can say, 'When I make a mistake, sometimes I feel *ashamed* – angry at myself and embarrassed – and it makes me want to hide. Do you ever feel that way?' Explaining emotions and helping your kid identify them opens up their ability to talk to you and God about it. The more you do this, the more you can encourage your kid to tell God everything, knowing that he understands all of those emotions.

Teenagers and prayer

KIRSTY S1E87

It was only when my own prayer life changed, when I realised God was trying to talk to me all the time, that the way I taught prayer to teenagers changed. We began to experiment, to listen and hang out with God – not always successfully, but sometimes dramatically and wonderfully.

We started with ten minutes. We would pose a question, like 'Ask God his favourite colour' or 'Ask God what he thinks about a particular situation'. It soon became obvious that ten minutes wasn't enough, so gradually this time got longer, becoming really precious. Parents would arrive and there'd be teenagers draped around the church, absolutely silent, because they were praying. It worked because it was their time with God. There were no rules. They were encouraged to walk around, write or draw pictures, and we had some remarkable answers to prayer.

Our jumping-off place was understanding that God loves them and if they were the only person in the world who'd messed up, Jesus would still have gone to the cross for them. Even if some of these young people didn't believe in God, just knowing that 'something' loved them meant they wanted to spend time with that 'something'.

We can help our teenagers pray by not telling them how to pray or by putting in rules. How you pray isn't going to be how they pray. So often teenagers will do the opposite of what you're doing, so allow them the freedom to explore God and their relationship with him in their own way. Anything goes. You can suggest things they might find helpful, but be laid-back and gentle. Be encouraged that God has got your teenager, despite appearances.

Follow-up

- 'Prayer' (p. 142) and 'Prayer – struggles and questions' (p. 153) chapters
- parentingforfaith.org/tool/chat-and-catch
- parentingforfaith.org/course – sessions 4 and 5 (Chat and catch)
- parentingforfaith.org/topics/prayer
- parentingforfaith.org/post/101-ways-to-start-a-conversation-with-god
- parentingforfaith.org/post/summary-prayer-and-under-fives

Next steps

- Do you recognise this idea of the high priest – maybe in the way people prayed with you as a child or how you pray with your children?
- How do you catch God's voice? Could you share that with your child?
- Do you think your kids know that they can pray informally or without using words?

P

PRAYER
STRUGGLES AND
QUESTIONS

RACHEL TURNER

Struggling to catch from God

`S1E99`

If you feel like you've explained chat and catch to your kid but they're still struggling, take a step back and look at their view of God. Session three of the Parenting for Faith course is about unwinding wrong views of God. Sometimes we teach our kids how to connect with God, but they don't want to, because they view God as angry, distant or not interested. Why would they want to connect with a God like that? It isn't necessarily something you've taught them; sometimes it's just how they've put together their life experience, Bible stories, what they heard from church and a random thing they saw in a movie. Very few children will be able to articulate their view of God, but often it'll pop up in different ways.

So ask questions that don't have a 'right' answer, like 'What do you think God did when he rested on the seventh day?' or 'What do you think God does while we're watching TV?' If you ask questions that have right answers, you're testing their knowledge. If you ask questions that don't have right answers, you're finding out how they view God, which may give you clues on what is making them feel so disconnected from God. If they're angry at God, encourage them to talk to God about their anger.

Also, take a moment to check your 'high priest' instinct, then tell your kid to connect with God in whatever way looks right for them – perhaps through nature, music or just lying silently on the ground. You can say, 'We want connecting time with God and it can be whatever. We don't have to do it together; I don't even have to be in the room. How do you want to connect with God and how can I help?' Hang in there, keep going; it's worth it to help your kids find their own path with God.

Unanswered prayer

S3E4

Helping our young people deal with disappointment is a key part of parenting. Sometimes they'll narrow down the idea of prayer to 'Did God do what I asked him to do?', as if God is a vending machine: 'I asked him to do this thing – he didn't do it, therefore he is not real.' This isn't something they'd ever do with you: 'I asked my parent to do something – they didn't do it; they don't exist.' That's not a realistic relational experience! God always responds to what we say. Sometimes he comforts us, sometimes he gives us an alternative ending to what we expected, sometimes he turns it for good and sometimes he leaves us in the struggle because he's shaping something in us.

So, for me, one of the questions is: 'Have you told God how you feel about that unanswered prayer?' It's okay to be disappointed or angry, and to ask him what he was doing. For a child who doesn't want to talk about it, do it in front of them or enable others who've been on the journey of processing unanswered prayer to share their stories with them.

Centring everything around God doing what we want him to do is not a biblical model of how we're to walk with God. But scripture does show us lots of ways people coped with the frustration and disappointment of unanswered prayer.

Why does God heal some and not others?

`S1E4`

Firstly, ask, 'What do you think?' We're all on a journey of figuring out what we think, and it's important that we give our kids space to communicate their thoughts, struggles and doubts – that's what faith is. Co-journeying with our kids is allowing them to say, 'I don't know and I don't like it', or, 'I don't know and it makes me angry.'

Secondly, what do we know? My answer would be:

- I know God can heal and does heal.
- I know God says to keep praying.
- I know one day, in the new heaven and new earth, there'll be no pain or disease.
- I know the world is still broken.

Thirdly, talk about what we *don't* know. I don't know how God chooses who to heal on earth. I don't think there's one simple answer to the secrets of God's heart on this.

Finally, share how you deal with it. My response: 'I've been so frustrated by this. I've had friends die even though I prayed – and other friends miraculously get better as we prayed. I cry, hope and keep telling God how I feel about it; I'm not afraid to tell him all my emotions. I ask him questions, pray for healing and ask for peace, that he would increase my hope and trust. In the end, I choose not to let seeing only a little piece of the whole puzzle rob me of doing life with God. I choose to be okay with not understanding, because I know one day there will be no more confusion or pain.'

You may disagree with my answer, and that's okay. However you choose to answer this question, asking your kids what they think, telling them what you know, showing them what you don't know and talking through how you deal with it opens up a helpful conversation.

Is chatting to God irreverent?

S1E102

Chatting to God and reverence towards God are aligned for two reasons. One is the positioning before God that the New Testament teaches us we have right now. When Jesus was talking about praying to God, he called him Abba, 'Father'. Children can share everything with their parents. This sense of sonship also pops up in Galatians and Romans.

In John 15:15, Jesus says, 'I no longer call you servants… Instead, I have called you friends.' This closeness is mind-blowing and awe-inspiring. Not only are we called children of God, but we are called friends. David says, 'Search me, God, and know my heart' (Psalm 139:23). This openness to God is what I see in chatting, completely aligned with what scripture tells us our position is to be.

The second reason is the nature of relationship. The more I get to know someone, the more I grow in reverence, honour and respect for them. Informality doesn't necessarily equal irreverence. Informality removes barriers between me and God, that I may see him clearly and hold nothing back. The more I see God clearly, the more I will grow in reverence. To me, the beauty of life with God is that I have the privilege of chatting to the God of the universe, holy beyond imagining, about someone saying something mean to me today. Chat orients itself in scripture as a conduit to more reverence. Reverence isn't in the language we use, but in the heart we have towards God.

Should kids memorise set prayers?

`S1E121`

The goal for our children is always to be able to communicate with God in their authentic voice. Some children feel that set prayers aren't the way they would naturally talk to God, so it becomes slightly disconnected for them.

But other children value having a jumping-in point for chatting to God – and for those children, set prayers can help them talk when they can't find the words. A memorised prayer can give children a starting point, from which to talk more to God about it. If your child would find that helpful, go for it. If you feel like their connection is going well, they might not need it right now. The most important thing is enabling our children to find what works for them in keeping authentically connected to God. And, as the parent, you will be able to see what's helping.

If you find set prayers useful in your own connection with God, that's a wonderful thing to create windows into for your children. Talk about it; let your kids see that you can talk informally with God but also sometimes use memorised prayers to help your heart find words. Frame it for your kids so they can see its richness and beauty.

Follow-up

- 'Prayer' (p. 142) and 'Prayer – chat and catch' (p. 148) chapters
- **parentingforfaith.org/course** – session 3 (Unwinding)
- **parentingforfaith.org/course** – sessions 4 and 5 (Chat and catch)
- **parentingforfaith.org/post/when-catch-is-hard**

Next steps

- How have you responded when your prayers haven't been answered in the way you would like? Could you create a window into that for your child?
- Are there any set prayers you use that help you move into conversational prayer with God?
- We all struggle with prayer at times – what to say or do, hearing God. Would it help your child to know of your struggles? How could you tell them?

P

PUBERTY

RACHEL TURNER AND EMMA WARING

Working out what you think

RACHEL S4E7

When it comes to puberty, we might worry that we're going to say or do the wrong thing, opening the door for our kids to mess up. We feel pressured to do it 'right', putting it down to a few awkward moments that we need to have with our kids and the 'right time' to have them.

But it's not just one conversation. As parents, we're discipling our kids as they grow up. Conversations about what's happening to your body are a part of life. When our kids are born, we have no problem talking about poo and wee; this is just another body thing that's happening. When we take away the awkwardness, it becomes a joy to help them through it.

Some of our awkwardness is because we haven't worked out what we think or how to explain it. So we can have those conversations with our partner and friends first, asking them what they think and having a go at explaining it.

Don't wait for the question or you'll end up trying to shove a lot of information into your kid all at once. Our job is to lay the framework for our kids, to give them the heads-up of what's coming regarding how their bodies are changing. You then get to set the narrative for their future: that you're excited for them to become a teenager and that you're going to be with them in it.

It's also helpful to frame for your kid how you're going to parent them in this season. Reassure them that you don't expect them to be perfect, but to learn from mistakes when they make them. Then they're not hiding from you but know they're safe in any circumstance. When they have questions, frame the importance of coming to you rather than Google by saying, 'I want you to ask me about it because I can give you the answer that you need.'

It's important that parents of both genders get clued up, because you may find that boys feel more comfortable talking to their mothers about body stuff, because their mothers are the ones who did a lot of the body stuff before. Or you may find that girls find it more comfortable talking to their dad. It's valuable to have a dad who understands what's happening to your body, that it's normal and not gross for men to know about.

God made our bodies. There's nothing that happens in your body that he is surprised by or grossed out by.

Building on good foundations

EMMA S7E4

We all love our children and want the best for them. When it comes to puberty, we can lay foundations which, as they grow, we can layer with more information. We know our children better than anyone else, so we have a duty to give them the best start in understanding these issues.

In my work with people experiencing sexual difficulties, one of the first questions I'll ask is about their upbringing. I ask them how they learnt where babies come from, how their parents talked about sex, or whether they talked about sex at all. What I've learned is that you give a message through *not* saying something just as much as through saying something negative. How we talk to our children will impact how they think about their bodies as sexual beings, so it's key that we are able to talk positively, which I recognise is not easy.

It is very usual for young children to enjoy touching their genitals. I certainly wouldn't use the term 'masturbation' here, because what they're doing is not a sexual thing; they're just enjoying exploring their bodies. But our response is key in terms of how they think about their genitals. We need to acknowledge that it can feel nice, but then talk about where might be appropriate for them to do that, i.e. a bedroom or bathroom.

When we see our five-year-old with their hands down their trousers in public, we might get a rising sense of panic and want them to stop. But this transmits our fear to them, and they feel they've done something naughty, dirty or shameful. You want to avoid that. It's worth checking out what's going on in yourself: *I feel panicked because I haven't had the conversation about appropriate touching, and now I've witnessed them do it in public and feel embarrassed.* Hold on to that: talk about it in a relaxed way when you get home. What I've heard from several patients is that their parents' panicked response shamed them. This can kickstart negative thinking about genitals, and it's important they're not picking that up. It's about being kind and curious with your child rather than critical.

Three years old is the typical age for children to ask where babies come from. We need to explain it in simple language. Sometimes children will ask questions that are difficult to answer, but the fact that they're inquisitive enough to ask means they'll be able to cope with an answer. The best approach is factual. What stumps most parents is talking about how the egg and seed meet. So let's imagine we've had conversations during bath time about penises and vaginas. You've had a conversation about how a baby is made, from a man's seed and a woman's egg. You say, 'When a man and a woman lie together and have a special type of cuddle, the man's penis is soft but when he lies with a woman it becomes hard because it feels nice. That's how it's been designed to be. When it's hard, it can go inside the woman's vagina and plant the seed.' As your child gets older, that language can develop.

Sadly, we needed to have conversations about pornography with our children from the age of seven, because that is the age many children get phones. Your own child might not have one, but they may be mixing with people who do. Talking about it is tricky, but we'd hate it if our kids were exposed without any vocabulary to say what they had seen. When we've given them a foundational understanding of sex, we can layer up their understanding about pornography, so they know they can talk to us if they see it. If they do, then ask how they felt about it, so you can validate their feelings and open up conversation. However difficult these conversations might be, we want our children to come to us – it's a privilege if they feel secure enough to ask this stuff because we've given them permission to talk to us about it.

The NSPCC estimates that one in 20 children will experience some form of sexual abuse under 16, and most by somebody they know. If we talk to our younger children about appropriate touching, if something untoward happens, they'll have the vocabulary to be able to tell us. It's sad, but we can't bury our heads in the sand. We live in the world that we live in, we need to be real and we need to protect our children so that they're able to say when something is wrong.

Follow-up

- 'Pornography' (p. 138) and 'Sex' (p. 179) chapters
- **parentingforfaith.org/post/summary-sex-and-puberty**
- **emmawaring.com**

Next steps

- Reflect on your own experience of puberty. Were there things you didn't know but should have? What would you like to do differently with your kids?
- Are conversations about puberty normal in your house? If not, how could you start those?
- What might be the next step for you and your child?

R

RACIAL EQUALITY

AZARIAH FRANCE-WILLIAMS AND RACHEL TURNER

Head, heart and hands

AZARIAH S7E7

As a black kid growing up in West Yorkshire, I did something which sociologists call 'code switching', where you move your language or register depending upon who you're with. I'd use a much flatter Yorkshire accent with my friends and a Caribbean accent with family and neighbours.

I didn't see many folks who reflected me in higher positions in society. I saw black sports stars and performers, but I didn't encounter black lawyers, doctors or police officers. It created an internal 'us and them' perspective. Some things are available to me and other things aren't. When my mum came to the UK with British qualifications in accountancy from her home island of Nevis, they were seen as null and void. She couldn't express her education and have that properly rewarded, so she did what she could to make ends meet for us, working as a receptionist and as a cleaner. She often encountered racism in the workplace and would talk to our church ministers about it. They'd offer prayer and comfort, but no action. If you're going to pray for someone, you have to be aware that God might want to use you as part of the answer!

Caribbean churches were often led by white aristocrats – those who'd gone the Eton-Oxbridge route and had a sense of the 'white man's burden'. Initially they went to the colonies for a jolly, but some of them made genuine relationships and began to learn and grow. When people were moving to the UK, they'd give them letters to take to the churches that they came to, but unfortunately when they arrived, the ministers were often so concerned about losing their white population that they often gave them a cold shoulder.

When I do racial justice training, I'll often ask people whether they've experienced being an outsider. They share a range of things, from having red hair to being neurodiverse. That becomes the empathy bridge to begin to talk about racial justice. Children might understand being an outsider if they're a bit shorter than other kids or they're not sporty, so use that as a way in.

Scripture is replete with outsiders, whether it's Ruth going with Naomi, Joseph being taken as a slave into Egypt, or Esther being taken into court. One of my favourites is Daniel and his friends; it's interesting to observe the degree to which they assimilate and adopt the new culture, and the degree to which they push back based on their religious, faith and cultural convictions.

Children do what we do, not always what we say. The biggest thing we can do as parents is to model it ourselves. Sometimes I ask people to list the five people they'll go to for advice. Often people are surprised that those they trust are people very much like them. That's not church, that's a club. The *ecclesia* – the Greco-Roman idea of the elite men of voting age who were able to make decisions on behalf of everybody else – was smashed, to include slaves, women and the marginalised. Sometimes, however, it's like we're going back to the original meaning.

In our internet age, there's no excuse for not being exposed to other cultures. We can listen to podcasts by black British content creators or read newspapers or children's magazines promoting stories of black young people, entrepreneurs and thinkers. We can go to places out of our comfort zone. Sometimes the majority culture likes to play host, but it's more uncomfortable playing the guest.

When your child encounters racism at school – perhaps to a classmate – think about it in terms of head, heart and hands:

- **Head** – When I've encountered racist behaviour and told somebody about it, sometimes they've questioned me, which makes me doubt myself. Although I pretty much know it was racist, the fact that the person isn't open to what I'm saying makes me retreat. Have the same openness that you would have if it were a member of your own family.

- **Heart** – God is love and we express God's love within the world, so how can we demonstrate a loving God within this situation? Perhaps you could organise a play date or park trip with the child who's been mistreated, to demonstrate kindness and begin to counter some of the rubbish that they've been absorbing.

- **Hands** – Sadly, those who should be taking responsibility don't always take it seriously, so you might need to go into the school and say something or ask about the school's policy. Theologian Walter Brueggemann says we only truly care about things when we take our bodies to them.

God's heart for justice

RACHEL S1E66

Every family has a different experience of racism. The question is: what is the next step for my child and how can I help them take it? Is it understanding the issue, engaging with God about it and letting this form their faith? Is it facilitating lament and prayer as they encounter stories of racism? Is it educating them about the historical and current situation? Is it seeking out the stories of others? Is it enabling their experiences to be heard in church?

You are their parent. Don't feel overwhelmed by the 'should': 'We *should* be sharing our stories as a family of colour' or 'We *should* be finding a home-school curriculum about racism.' Pause and ask God for the next step, whether it's prayer, activism or education.

Then take this opportunity to disciple your child in God's heart for justice. Justice is a key aspect of who God is and what he commands us to seek.

We want to train our kids to look to God to constantly realign their hearts: expressing pain, exposing sin and readjusting their ways of thinking. Teach them to find God's heart and align themselves with that, so that they know what he feels about it, what he is doing and what he calls us to. You can do that by accessing scripture, finding books and just talking about it together.

Follow-up

- A.D.A. France-Williams, *Ghost Ship: Institutional racism and the Church of England* (SCM Press, 2020)
- parentingforfaith.org/post/how-can-we-talk-to-our-children-and-teens-about-injustice

Next steps

- What could you do to widen your child's exposure to other cultures?
- How might you help your child explore God's heart for justice and what that means when we encounter racism?
- 'If you're going to pray for someone, you have to be aware that God might want to use you as part of the answer!' Wonder as a family if God is asking you to be part of the answer.

R

RE LESSONS

RACHEL TURNER S1E49

Sometimes RE lessons can be a difficult place to be. There are two things here: 1) how to handle an aggressive environment faith-wise, and 2) how to help our children answer difficult questions. Sometimes we squish them together, feeling like we need to equip our kids to answer questions so that they can handle aggressive environments – but they are two separate issues. They can inform each other, but when we think about them separately, then we can become more proactive and helpful.

The first thing I would suggest is to help our children handle an aggressive environment faith-wise. It can be tough to feel like the one kid responsible for all of Christianity's answers. Everybody is different: some kids hate to be exposed in that group environment, while others love the challenge. The interesting conversation is not 'How can we deal with aggressive people?' but 'Who do I feel called to be in this environment?' Our job as a parent is to help them ask that question, because they're going to have to ask it in every school and workplace they find themselves.

If they don't want to be exposed in that environment, that's okay. You can come up with ways of getting them out of that, phrases they can use (like 'I don't know but I still believe' or 'I don't know – that's a tough one isn't it?'), or how to listen and give an 'I don't know' answer. Create windows into how you do it, but also equip them. If your kid wants to research questions and come equipped every week for a new question, you can do that together. If they want to be able to talk about their faith without pressure, then you can talk to the teacher together.

Secondly, we can talk about how to answer the actual question. Does your kid actively have that question? Or do they just feel like they *should* know the answer? You can equip them more in apologetics; some questions do have answers and some of them are wide open. There is such a rich experience of apologetics, of saying: 'These are the answers we know, these are the answers people are still wrestling with and this is how they got there theologically.' Follow your kid's curiosity, rather than feeling like there's a tick box of things that you have to shove into their head.

It's also important to help your kid cope with the fact that doubt is okay and you don't have to know the answers to have a faith. Normalising wondering is an important part of this journey for children, because they need to know that Christianity isn't just knowing all the things on the list; it's a walk with God.

Follow-up

- 'Big questions' (p. 35), 'Doubt' (p. 70) and 'School' (p. 171) chapters
- **parentingforfaith.org/post/intellectual-wrestlers-equipping-kids-who-need-to-know**
- **parentingforfaith.org/post/summary-faith-and-school**

Next steps

- What's your child's experience of RE lessons? Do they feel exposed as a Christian?
- How could you help them think about or prepare for tricky questions?
- Share stories of your experiences in RE lessons or times when you've felt put on the spot by someone's questions. What did you do? How do you feel about that now?

S

SANTA

LUCY RYCROFT AND RACHEL TURNER

St Nicholas

LUCY S1E50

In our family we talk about Santa as St Nicholas, so that's how we 'get round' the Santa thing. But it's more than that: it's an intrinsic part of our Advent celebrations. It's not just about how we put up with Santa, but about bringing Santa – or St Nicholas – into our celebrations.

St Nicholas was a real person. He loved God, and though he didn't have much, he lived generously in his community, gave to the poor, and gave his time and his love. That's such a good picture of Jesus and what we're celebrating at Christmas. St Nicholas had so little but he devoted his life to serving his community, and his example is such a great one to share with our children at Christmas.

So when we talk about Santa, we say he was a real person, he was St Nicholas and we celebrate him as Santa. He's gone to be with Jesus now, but he was a real person and we can keep his memory alive as we 'do' Santa.

Using Santa to unwind wrong views of God

RACHEL SIE93

At Parenting for Faith, we often talk about 'unwinding' wrong views of God. Our children put together their view of God from experiences, movies, what we tell them, what the Bible tells us, and what church tells them, and they combine it altogether into how they view God. We tend to compare God to people that we know, so whether or not you choose to play the Santa game with your kids, Santa opens up an interesting opportunity to ask, 'How are God and Santa similar? What are the differences?'

Sometimes our children conflate the two. For instance, the song 'Santa Claus is coming to town' tells us that Santa sees you when you're sleeping and knows when you're awake. A lot of children think the exact same thing about God, that he is watching and judging our behaviour, which can lead to them thinking that God deals with us in the same way that Santa does.

You can see how kids get confused. Santa is described as omnipresent, omniscient and miraculous. He loves you, gives good gifts, is jolly and delightful. He has elves that put his miraculous plans into action; God has angels. This can lead to some interesting conversations. For example, if you're good Santa gives you good things, and if you're bad he gives you bad things. Is God like that? Does God look at our behaviour and give good things to people who do good things and bad things to people who do bad things? Or maybe it's about how God doesn't give us what we deserve but what his Son deserves – and then you're into sin and grace.

You could have other conversations about how Santa is watching and judging you from the outside, whereas God knows your heart and walks with you in relationship. Santa doesn't want to be seen and known, but God sent Jesus so we can know him better. Santa gives us gifts to make us happy; God's plan for our lives is not simply to make us happy but to transform us to become more like God. Santa gives you gifts once a year, but God has said there are many gifts he is constantly wanting to give you.

Follow-up

- 'Advent' (p. 10) and 'Christmas' (p. 40) chapters
- **thehopefilledfamily.com** (Lucy Rycroft)
- **parentingforfaith.org/post/how-do-we-decide-how-to-approach-father-christmas**

Next steps

- How have you talked about Santa in your family?
- What role (if any) does he play in your celebrations? What else is important to your family at Christmas?
- If Santa is part of your Christmas, how can you keep Jesus as the highlight of the season?

S

SCHOOL

RACHEL TURNER

Preparing our children for a non-Christian world

S1E28

Often we want to protect our kids from others not understanding their faith. But in John 16, Jesus preps his disciples for hard situations, assuring them that the Holy Spirit will help them, finishing by saying, 'I have told you these things, so that in me you may have peace' (John 16:33). We often get sucked into thinking that people won't understand our Christianity, so we'll need to defend it. But defence *isn't* a helpful place to start. Here are three alternatives.

Firstly, explain that not everyone knows God. That can be a new concept for kids; not everyone knows God the way we do, so they may be confused or have questions. When it comes up, you can just talk about it like everything else you would talk about.

Secondly, if your child is getting flak, equip them to talk about their faith rather than making them the ultimate defender of all Christianity. Most of the time, kids just need some encouragement to not worry about having all the answers, but to be able to say, 'I know God is real because…' Some kids love apologetics and we can equip them, but it's about enabling *your* kid to be authentic and share their understanding of the hope that they have.

Thirdly, create windows into your life of how you live, and have lived, in the world with people who don't understand your faith. Sharing your stories of encounters with non-Christian friends and colleagues is helpful.

Choosing a secondary school

S1E57

Choosing a secondary school is a massive deal, and I completely understand the stress, particularly when you feel strongly about one particular school. You are the expert in your child and know what's best for them, so here are some approaches to help you find your way forward.

Firstly, consider why you want your child to go to this particular school. What are you hoping they'll get out of it or what will it protect them from? Often we, as parents, can't articulate why we want something, so it doesn't sound convincing when we tell our kids. Particularly as they get older, kids want justifications for our opinions, so put some time into thinking about why this school is important. Then you can explain to them how this school fulfils the things you think are essential for them and how a different choice would mean looking at how those things would be integrated into their life, as the school wouldn't be providing them.

Secondly, recognise the importance of your child's friendships. The move to secondary school represents a huge change for them, and friends are important. It could be that your child doesn't make friends easily or that they have a few deep friendships, so their main source of support and companionship is these people. While you can never guarantee that today's friends will be future friends, your child needs to hear that you value their friendships and recognise their importance. It can't be the main reason for your choice, but adding it to the 'plus' side of the decision columns will help your child feel understood.

Thirdly, help your child explore what is important to them in a school. What do they need in school to flourish? You can add your ideas, and then make a master list of what you'll be judging these schools on.

Finally, model how a decision is made with God. This is an important skill for your child to learn. You can ask God for guidance together, and do some chatting and catching. Explore together what God is communicating to each of you. Talk about how you've made decisions in life and how God's guidance can make us feel peaceful, so God is an important part of figuring this out. When you visit schools, pray before you go in and chat afterwards about how you felt God was nudging you when you were in there.

At the end of all of this exploration, by the time you decide which school is right, you will both know why and what God is going to do. By guiding your child on the journey, they will feel empowered, rather than just submitting to you because you're the parent.

Disagreeing with school

S1E92

What do you do when your child's school is teaching from a different value system to you?

Often, we feel powerless and worried, like we're in a push-and-pull competition with the school. But you can grab your power back, because you don't need to feel confused and disempowered.

Find out what is being taught. Children don't always accurately report what they're learning; sometimes they get stuff mixed up. So rather than kick down the school door, go in with an open, kind heart and ask what they're teaching and how. Explain that you want to know how to prep your kid for it. You're happy for them to teach the curriculum but want to help frame for your kid how it fits into the wider narrative of the value system you hold. Often they'll want to hear your concerns and respect you too. You're not saying the school or teacher needs to change, you're saying you want as much information as possible to help your kid manage this experience.

You may choose to leave it there or you may choose to wade into it with your kid. You can say, 'I understand that school is teaching this, and there are bits I agree with, and other bits I don't, because they don't know God the way I know God. They say "Christians think this" but I know because this is my life and I live it.'

Sometimes you'll disagree with what school is saying. This gives you a chance to frame how it's okay to exist in a space where others think differently. You can talk about how you cope with that, how you protect your mind, how you can be gracious and non-judgemental. This is how we cope in a world that doesn't always agree with us. And that's a great discipleship journey to go on.

No matter what the school is teaching, find out exactly what's being taught, figure out what you think and what is developmentally appropriate to wade into at this time with your kid, then help them understand what you agree and don't agree with. Talk about how we walk as Christians in humility, boldness and love, bringing God to all situations. There's no need to be afraid of the school, because as the parent you have deep influence in your kid's life. And to your child, you're showing them what life looks like as a Christian in a world that has different values to us.

Follow-up

- 'RE lessons' (p. 166) chapter
- parentingforfaith.org/tool/chat-and-catch
- parentingforfaith.org/post/transitions
- parentingforfaith.org/post/talking-to-kids-about-decision-making
- parentingforfaith.org/post/summary-faith-and-school

Next steps

- What's your child's experience of being a Christian in an environment where others aren't?
- If you are looking at choosing a new school, which of Rachel's suggestions do you find helpful?
- If you disagree with anything school is teaching, what does your child need to help them navigate it well?

S

SCIENCE AND GOD

RACHEL TURNER AND DR LIZ COLE

A conflict between science and faith?

RACHEL S1E18

If your kids believe there's a conflict between science and faith, dig around to discover where they got the idea that science is contrary to faith. Science is a window into the amazingness of God, the investigation of the creativity of God's design. Only God can weave together a vast natural world. If your kids believe science is totally different to faith, there's a big foundational shift that needs to happen.

Start by finding Christian scientists, maybe in your church, and invite them over. Have them talk about how they reconciled science and faith. Find out what actual questions your kids have and create windows into how you cope with them.

Find Christians who love science. Louie Giglio has written a couple of fascinating children's devotionals about what different aspects of science reveal to us about God. I would dive into the books with the kids, because it would help engage them on an intellectual level. We can say, 'That's fascinating, isn't it? I don't know the answer, but this is what it looks like for me. Let's invite some people over who love God and love science, and talk about it.'

Creation versus evolution

RACHEL S1E34

At school, our children are taught about evolution, yet we read them Bible stories that describe creation in a seemingly day-by-day timeframe. How do we help our kids reconcile that? We have four steps to answer this question. (See 'Big questions' chapter.)

1 **What do you think?** Get them talking to figure out where the question is coming from.

2 **What do we know?** We know that God created the world: it's what scripture says, and it's who we see in the character of God. He is a creator; everything comes from him.

3 **What do we not know?** We don't know *how* he created the world. The Bible says he did it in seven days. Is that an actual day or a long chunk of time? Different people have different opinions.

4 **Share how you've handled this.** My answer would be: 'I keep going back to the fact that God is beyond my understanding. He made the world, but exactly how, I don't know. He gave me a story of how he did it, and whether I believe that literally or figuratively, I still fundamentally believe that God made the world. I believe that science is a way that I can understand God better, a window into his awesomeness. So when scientists say something, I listen. Sometimes I agree and sometimes I don't, but that's okay, because in the end God made everything, and how he made it is up to him.'

Regardless of how you choose to answer, make sure you share how it looks in your life and how it turns your heart to God.

Being a scientist and a Christian

LIZ S8E2

As a young Christian at university, I joined the Christian Union. The Bible teaching was good, but I detected a fear of science. It was a mystery to me, because there'd been no conflict between faith and science in my own understanding. This faction within the church, which insisted that the Bible was almost a scientific textbook as well as God telling us who he is, bothered me.

So I attended a course on science and faith – and it was wonderful. It was a huge comfort to find that an awful lot of very clever scientists who are atheists as young adults, as they research more and more, conclude that the only possible explanation is God. It irritates them enormously and they become Christians! Everything from geology to astronomy, carbon dating, the formation of elements – every part of our creation points to a God who made it.

While I was on this journey, The Faraday Institute for Science and Religion-funded a survey of school children. They found that children as young as five think that God and science have nothing to do with each other. Even worse, they found that by the time children are leaving primary school, this morphs into a view that science is the 'real world' and God has nothing to do with it. That's the stark picture of why it's so important, as Christians, to know how big God is and the extreme lengths he's prepared to go to in his love for us. If all the different sciences were made by God, then they're a manifestation of God just as the Bible is. So they can't be conflicting; it might just be that science is telling us the what, how and when, and the Bible is telling us the who and the why.

When we read the way the universe was created – the 'natural world' – as God's word, as well as the Bible, it doesn't explain huge issues like suffering, but it throws light on them. God chose to make a physical, material universe. We're spiritual beings as well, and God obviously made the spiritual world, but the realm of science is limited to the physical, material world. Science has fundamental laws, one of which is that everything tends to decay. Why did the meteorite strike the earth? Imagine the suffering of those creatures that got splatted first and then suffered a slow and painful end because of the nuclear winter effect that followed. But if you don't have a planet, you can't have life. Because the planet formed, we can get life, and that life can evolve and grow. It's not so much that the clouds have silver linings, but that the silver linings have clouds. Connecting with God through the Bible and through his creation helps us understand science.

Follow-up

- 'Big questions' (p. 35) and 'RE lessons' (p. 166) chapters
- **parentingforfaith.org/post/intellectual-wrestlers-equipping-kids-who-need-to-know**
- Elizabeth Cole, *God's Cosmic Cookbook: Your complete guide to making a universe* (John Murray Press, 2023)
- Louie Giglio, *Indescribable: 100 devotions about God and science* (Tommy Nelson, 2017)
- Louie Giglio, *How Great Is Our God: 100 indescribable devotions about God and science* (Tommy Nelson, 2019)
- **faraday.cam.ac.uk**

Next steps

- What big questions does your child have about science and God?
- Does your child assume that science and faith are incompatible? How could you find out what they think?
- Who or what might help your child or teen dig into the relationship between faith and science?

S

SEX

SHEILA WRAY GREGOIRE S7E5

One problem with the way Christians sometimes think about sex is that it's something which men need and women provide.

When we surveyed 7,000 women for our book *She Deserves Better* to find out how the messages they heard as teens affected them long-term, it was sad. It's going to be difficult to get it right if we're still holding on to unhelpful things we were taught. We may see sex as something fundamentally scary and threatening; in its proper place, it's beautiful. God created sex to be mutual, pleasurable and intimate; it's sacred and meaningful.

Often with boys we assume that sex is all they think about; we treat them like they can't help it, like they're little lust monsters. A couple of years ago a viral Facebook post told of a woman who walked into church with her teenage boys. Some teenage girls wearing leggings walked in and sat in the pew in front of them, so this woman's family went and sat in front of them, so that her boys wouldn't be distracted by these girls during worship. But what lesson did she teach her boys? She taught them that it's impossible for them to think about God or remain in a good headspace when there are attractive girls around. She's taught them that they're helpless.

What if you simply acted like it's no big deal? You're going to see people you find attractive sometimes, and you can move on. Noticing is not lusting – but we've taught boys and girls that if a guy notices a woman's body, he's already sinned. That's an awful burden to put on teenage boys, because how are they supposed to not notice? Multiple studies have found that boys who are hypervigilant about this, who have a very shame-based message about lust, are more likely to struggle with pornography or less likely to have healthy relationships with girls. So teach both your boys and your girls that they will see attractive people, and it doesn't have to be a big deal.

If you're in a good marriage, display your affection publicly if you can: hold each other's hands, because it lets your kids see that you like each other and enjoy touching each other. You don't want your kids to think marriage is where sex goes to die!

Think about how often in scripture it says, 'Do not be afraid.' So many of us are afraid of the sex conversation, and we blow it up in our minds. We think that if our kids know certain words they're going to act on them, so we don't want to explain it because it'll ruin their innocence. Let me tell you emphatically, that's not true. What we found was that the more words about sex that girls knew when they graduated high school, the less likely they were to engage in risky sexual behaviours or have multiple sexual partners. Information is very protective, because if they know they can get it from you they won't look for it elsewhere. If they can name these sexual activities, then they'll understand what others are talking about, so they're not as likely to get drawn in. It also makes it much harder to abuse kids when they have words for things they can talk to you about.

We need to teach our kids a sexual ethic that endures throughout their life, whether married or single: 'I will use my body to love and honour other people, and I will always treat others with dignity.' Instead of teaching a sexual ethic of 'You don't do anything sexual when you're single and then once you're married anything goes' – no, you're always going to use your body to love and honour others, and you're always going to treat others with dignity. That's what Jesus did.

This means that when you're single, you're going to treat others with dignity. Having sex at 15 often has long-term consequences, and you don't want to do that to someone that you're probably not going to marry. Especially for girls, sex is not necessarily a physically pleasurable experience early on. For boys, you don't want to cause a girl's discomfort or pain, just so that you can get some pleasure, do you? That's not treating her with dignity.

Treating others with dignity also means that if a girl comes up scantily dressed, you still treat her with dignity. The lust message is about trying to control what girls are wearing, but you're never going to be able to control what every girl in the world is wearing, so the emphasis has to be that, no matter what she's wearing, you treat her with dignity. Tell girls the same thing about boys – that you're capable of treating them with dignity. Let's believe in our kids, because kids rise to expectations.

One important thing kids need to know is the concept of arousal non-concordance – the idea that your brain and body don't necessarily match up. Your body could feel aroused when your brain doesn't like what's happening. It's important because if someone is a victim of date rape or sexual assault, but in the process became aroused, they often feel like they consented and it was their fault. When we teach that arousal does not equal consent, that's huge – especially for boys, because sex anatomically can't happen unless there's an erection. That's also important for the porn conversation. Many kids will see pornography which is violent and degrading, and they're completely grossed out – but their body responds, so they think they like it, and start seeking it out. Tell your kids ahead of time that when you see stuff designed to arouse you, it doesn't mean you're an addict. You can walk away and this doesn't define you.

Follow-up

- 'Pornography' (p. 138) and 'puberty' (p. 158) chapters
- parentingforfaith.org/post/summary-sex-and-puberty
- Sheila Wray Gregoire, *She Deserves Better: Raising girls to resist toxic teachings on sex, self, and speaking up* (Baker Publishing Group, 2023)
- sheilawraygregoire.com

Next steps

- What messages about sex did you grow up with? How have these affected you?
- What do your children think about sex? What messages might they be hearing from church or Christians, and what from the world around them?
- What of Sheila's advice might you want to share with your child and when?

S

SHAME

Shame – that sense of stuff being on your heart, even though you've been forgiven – is a reality for children as well as adults. There's a difference between conviction and shame. Conviction is God exposing our sin so that we can repent and come close to him again. But shame is when we allow our judgement of ourselves to keep us in that place of pain and separation. It makes us want to hide from God because we feel unworthy of his forgiveness.

When we see our children get trapped in shame, it can be hard to know what to do. But if we keep an eye on them and notice when they are feeling ashamed, we can teach them valuable life skills of how to cope with it. I'm going to pull four ideas from the six-stage circle – you can find more about this in the surfing the waves episode of our free Parenting for Faith course.

Firstly, create windows. Shame is usually something that we hide, so our children rarely know we struggle with it. Every so often, we can strategically share a glimpse of our inner life with our children. We might say, 'I've been trying to speak well of a person at work, even though they're mean, but I slipped today and God poked my heart. I knew I was wrong and God cleaned my heart – but it's been a battle today to not let shame climb into me and make me want to hide because I'm embarrassed.' It doesn't have to be that long, it can be a sentence, but just something to make our kids aware that sometimes our brains and hearts do that.

Secondly, frame it. Shame is hard for kids to articulate. They need us to say, 'If we're feeling like we want to hide from God after we clean up our mess, that's called shame. God tells us in the Bible that that's not how he wants us to live. When he says we're forgiven, we are. There is no need to feel embarrassed or heavy in our hearts anymore.' Kids don't need to live with that embarrassment or struggle with anger at themselves for not being perfect. It's helpful to pivot their brain by being grateful for forgiveness and that we don't have to be perfect, rather than beating ourselves up about our mistakes. We can also frame how shame affects people in TV shows and movies or how people in the Bible dealt with it (like Paul, who had a massively sinful past). People made lots of mistakes in the Bible and they had to learn how to walk with what they had done, living free in their heart before God.

Thirdly, equip your children to deal with shame. You can suggest they chat with God about it, or if you think they haven't yet sorted the sin out with God, you can say, 'I always feel better when I ask God to take away that heavy feeling, because he always does.' You can notice when your child is withdrawing, and ask them whether they might be feeling embarrassed or upset with themselves. You can then understand and hear their feelings. If they're getting stuck on certain thoughts or phrases, you can help them create truth swaps; for example, when they think, 'I'm so dumb for doing that', swap it with, 'That's a tough hill to climb but I'm getting better.' You are the expert in your kid. What equipping do they need to handle those thoughts?

Fourthly, create opportunities for your child to remind *you* of the truth. You could say, 'My brain keeps reminding me of mistakes I made and it makes me feel sad. What are some good truths that need to go in my heart?' or 'Can you pray for me again?' This isn't making your kid your accountability partner or the receiver of all of your emotions, but once in a while, there is real value in allowing them to engage with what that aspect of life with God looks like for you. It's also a great opportunity to ask them about their life.

Starting with those four steps means we can begin to establish within our family culture that shame is a normal part of the life God came to free us from.

Follow-up

- 'Grace' (p. 103) and 'Sin' (p. 189) chapters
- parentingforfaith.org/post/summary-sin-forgiveness-and-salvation
- parentingforfaith.org/post/the-six-stage-circle
- parentingforfaith.org/course

Next steps

- Do you find the way Rachel defines shame helpful?
- Does your child feel shame? What help might they need to understand what they are feeling?
- How can you create windows into how shame affects you and how God helps?

SIBLING RIVALRY

OLLY GOLDENBERG AND RACHEL TURNER

How can you encourage siblings to be good friends?

OLLY S4E3

Be encouraged that sibling rivalry is found right in the very beginning – the very first siblings in the Bible (Cain and Abel) had a severe rivalry going on. Why is it going on? Because those closest to us are those whom we feel most comfortable to be ourselves around, but also because we can feel in competition with our siblings. So one of the things we try to do with our children is to help them appreciate each other's strengths. They always may want to do better than each other, but helping them begin to appreciate and celebrate what the other person is good at can start to take the edge off any rivalry.

The other thing for us as parents is to watch our children not just in the home, but outside the home when others are about. For me, this is the litmus test of how big an issue it is, because if they're defending each other outside the home and fighting each other in the home, then we're probably okay and going to come through this. But if they're speaking badly against each other outside the home, then that's something we need to talk through. We're family, we have to stick up for each other whether we like it or not. That's something we want to feed into our children.

When siblings fight

RACHEL S1E15

You can't make your children love each other, but you can help them figure out how to be a blessing to each other. As parents of siblings, we can spend lots of our time negotiating behaviours. Every once in a while, it helps to stop and have conversations about our hearts, because in essence you're discipling your kids in how to have a healthy relationship with somebody else. It might not be the closest relationship in the world, but it is a basic relationship.

You can talk about firstly what's happening in themselves. If, for example, they say, 'When my brother took my toy, I got so angry I just wanted to hit him', then you can say that's an emotion we all have in common. We can help coach them through that anger by asking:

- What do you do when you have those emotions?
- What does it do to your relationship when you choose to act out of your anger rather than a conversation?
- What happens to your heart when you're willing to hurt somebody else?
- How do you fix that relationship when you've done something that has broken your trust and connection?

Secondly, you can talk about the other person. For example, 'Taking your sister's toy made her feel very powerless, which is an awful feeling and makes people feel very protective. So how can you do something to share our power, so that we can take care of each other's hearts and live peacefully?'

When you help your child process what's going on in their hearts and help them fix the relationship with their sibling, that can be more helpful than just coming in and sorting out the decision part of the discipline. The other part is that we need to fix our relational mess:

- How are you going to rebuild trust?
- How are you going to fix your hurt feelings so that you're not brooding on them?

It doesn't have to be every time that you work this out, but it is helpful in conversation to help them learn how to manage their own hearts and their relationships when you have the energy. Sometimes it can be a long time after the conflict. Sometimes just sort out behaviour and then at bedtime have the conversation. But those conversations are helpful to call back to memory next time someone's taking someone's toy, as you can say, 'It looks like you're getting angry, how are you going to cope with that?', or, 'Excuse me, we let everybody have power in this family. How can you use both of your powers well so that we're taking care of everybody's heart in relationship?'

Follow-up

- 'Emotions' (p. 82) and 'New siblings' (p. 129) chapters
- **childrencan.co.uk** (Olly Goldenberg)
- **parentingforfaith.org/post/helping-our-children-develop-character-through-sibling-rivalry**

Next steps

- If your children struggle with their siblings, what ideas from this chapter might you want to try?
- Rachel suggests there are two steps: to sort out the decision part of the problem and also to fix the relational mess. Do you find that helpful?
- What are the next steps for you and your children?

S

SIN

RACHEL TURNER

A healthy, holistic view of sin

S1E106

We all need Jesus. Our kids need to know how to access him and deal with sin in a way that's right. So here are three thoughts about having a holistic view of sin.

Firstly, sin isn't the reason to have a relationship with God; it's the barrier in that relationship. If we can be positive about what life with God looks and feels like, creating windows into the beauty of a life lived with God, then sin is the stumbling block, the wall we run into. Jesus has dealt with it. God has provided a way to get rid of it without us having to be perfect, and it's great. If sin has its proper place, then our life with God isn't focused on our sin, but on who he is.

Secondly, we often get confused about how God feels about sin, which means God comes across as angry and disgusted with all humans. In reality, God deeply loves us and seeks us out. He created us for relationship and grieves when we choose sin and disconnection, providing ways back so that we don't have to live disconnected. He is angry about sin because it's a barrier between him and his child.

Finally, it's helpful to teach children how to handle sin in their life – how to notice when they're sinning, bring it to God and move on – as part of normal everyday life as opposed to a big crisis. Model that in your own life, so that sin is recognised as a barrier for a beautiful relationship with God that we can access in everyday life.

Explaining sin

S1E104

The topic of sin can feel like such a big deal to work up to in our discipleship of our kids. But if we can weave it into our normal everyday conversations, we are showing our kids that it's a normal cycle of life. We can have an encounter, receive forgiveness, feel connected and move on. We want them to find God, forgiveness and freedom in their ordinary everyday. Here are my suggestions for how we can do that.

Firstly, create windows. Most of our faith is private, particularly confession, but there are moments when kids need to see what to do. You don't have to do that every day, just every so often. Let your kids see what it looks like to feel convicted and to say sorry for something you've done. You can do it when you snap at them and apologise, but also explain that you need to sort that out with God too. Kids often don't have a language for what sin feels like. As adults, rather than simply saying 'I kicked Jesus in the shins', we can give a more expansive explanation such as, 'I didn't behave in the way Jesus would have done. I'm disconnected from God, which is not how I want to live.'

Secondly, weave in the concept of what sin does. For example, you could say: 'As a family, we're connected to each other; there's nothing between us. When we don't operate in love, something happens to our connection, and that person then separates a bit.' Integrate this as part of talking about how when you apologise and acknowledge sin, you can get forgiveness and come close together. Point out that they have opportunities to remove everything between them and God and run back to him, because Jesus provided the concept of reconnection so that it can be in your relationships.

Thirdly, tell the whole story of sin. I would say that we were created to live with God, always aware of his presence, always feeling loved, confident and comfortable in who he made us to be and what he asks us to do. At some point, people chose to live differently. They made a decision that moved God's love out of the centre of their choices. When they did that, other things began to power their decisions and that disconnected them from God. But he provided Jesus so that all our mistakes could be swept away, and we could live in that connection with him, as he teaches us how to have love at the centre again. That's how I describe it – you may describe it differently – but it gives an idea of how sin plays out, its consequences and how it works out.

Finally, remember there are so many opportunities to coach our children in this cycle of coming to God. There may be times when your kids come home and you can sense they are carrying shame. You might say, 'When I feel like that, sometimes I just need to tell God about it. Do you want to do that? Is that something you'd like help with?' Your kid may want you to coach them through it, and you can say, 'This is how I tell God what I did. Why don't you do that now in your head? I don't need to hear it I'm just here to help you and God connect.' And your kid can chat to God in the privacy of their own mind, and when they're done you can say, 'Why don't you tell God whatever you want to about fixing that relationship?' Then you might ask if they want to chat to God, say thank you or sing a worship song. Your kid may say, 'I'm done', or 'Go away, I want more time with God' – but you've coached your kids through it, rather than just saying, 'Say sorry to God. Great, you're done.' This isn't just about saying sorry; this is about a process of reconciliation, of creating space for that to happen. However your kid needs it, equip them to have that individual encounter for themselves.

Overly focused on sin?

S3E9

If your child is overly worried about sin and feels the need to repeatedly say sorry to God, it might be because they're feeling afraid of him. Sometimes there's a root in there that's helpful to dig out, so if it's because they're afraid that if they don't say sorry enough something bad's going to happen, you can begin to unwind that. Ask them to tell you more, then you can begin to understand.

Or it could be that they see God as someone who's constantly upset with them. It could be that they've never been coached in how to access and embrace forgiveness. It could be that in your relationship with your kids, it takes you a while to get over their sin, and so they feel like they have to keep saying sorry until you're happy again. You can reassure them that God's much better at this than you are, and so when we sin he separates it and is still there with us. The issue here is probably not so much about sin but the reconciliation process.

The power of the apology

S1E54

Our children aren't perfect and neither are we. When we get used to apologising well, we create an opportunity to show them how to handle their mistakes. We often try to enforce their apologies, but a key thing we can do is show them how to apologise by doing it ourselves.

If you do something you need to apologise for, give the 'gold star level' apology. Rather than just saying, 'I'm sorry for yelling', go for the long explanation of what's going on in your heart: 'I'm so sorry that I rushed you until you felt stressed. I was feeling embarrassed and angry because I'd made mistakes in getting myself ready, and I wanted to be on time. I rushed you so we could get out quickly, which was unfair on you. I'm sorry I made you feel upset. I'm still learning how to get everybody ready on time, and I didn't do it right today. Will you forgive me? I'm going to chat to God about it but wanted to fix my mess with you too.'

Many parents report that when they up their apology game, modelling all those bits of understanding and affirmation, they begin to see their children change towards each other, apologising genuinely, more frequently and without being prompted. Just by changing how they, as parents, apologise, they show their kids that it's not about resentfully saying 'I'm sorry', but understanding the other person and saying what you're going to change.

There's something fun about sharing stories, as a family, of when you messed up, whether recently or in the past. It's a joyful sharing, which normalises the process of becoming more and more like who God has made us to be, but it also shows where God was in all of our messes. Every moment of parenting is an opportunity to show our children where God is in the mess and how to engage with each other and him.

Follow-up

- 'Grace' (p. 103) and 'Shame' (p. 183) chapters
- parentingforfaith.org/post/summary-sin-forgiveness-and-salvation

Next steps

- Are there any ideas that are new for you in this chapter?
- How does your child understand 'sin'? How do you know? What else might they need to know?
- How could you coach your child in how to handle sin in their life?

SOCIAL MEDIA

RACHEL TURNER AND BECKY SEDGWICK

Getting our heads around social media

RACHEL S1E31

Social media can be scary; there's so much out there and it keeps changing. There's a series of questions to ask ourselves when it comes to getting our brains around social media.

The first is: 'Am I ready?' You don't have to be super savvy, but you do have to know enough to coach your kids through it. It's okay to pause your kid's engagement with social media until you feel ready to keep them safe. I recommend Care for the Family's book *Left to Their Own Devices?* – or take a youth pastor or young adult out to dinner and ask them to talk you through what's on their phone to get an idea of what your child might be encountering.

The second question is: 'Is my kid ready?' Just because other kids are using social media doesn't mean yours has to. You get to choose what they engage with and when. Social media is a warped reality. It can remove responsibility in interpersonal relationships, create unrealistic standards, and open your kid up to judgement and manipulation, as well as predators. When kids learn how to swim, we don't just throw them in the deep end. The same applies to digital stuff. How is our kid in dealing with other people's judgements? How well do they understand manipulation? Do they understand what to do when they see something you don't want them to see? If you think they're ready, then great. If not, then it's okay to say no or to restrict their access as you train them in the skills.

You are the expert in how your kid is, how their heart works and how their character is developing. Learning about social media is just information that you can acquire. Parenting your kids through it draws mostly on your knowledge about your kid. Once you know enough about this new realm, you can apply your already good parenting to it.

Discipling our kids around social media

BECKY S1E117

How can we proactively and usefully disciple a kid in how to live well in the world of social media when we know less than they do? There are three things about God's love that can help us help our kids navigate social media.

Firstly, God's love is unconditional. God wants us to do everything in a way that's good for us, whether that's playing football, watching television or going shopping. He doesn't want to see us hurt or damaged. So the first thing to help our kids understand is that when we engage with social media, we want to do it in a way that is good and healthy for us. Frame your own use of social media so they understand how you make decisions. What sites do you no longer visit? How do you choose what to post or share? Ask your kids questions: why do you think people follow social media crazes? Why do you think this app has a 13-years age restriction? Help them see you're interested in them using social media in a way that's good for them. Equip your kids to think critically about what they see: is this something God would want me to see, hear, feel or do? Philippians 4:8 is a helpful standard to hold things up to: 'Whatever is true, noble, right, pure, lovely, admirable – if anything is excellent or praiseworthy – think about such things.'

Secondly, God wants us to partner with him in sharing his love with others. There are lots of ways we can use social media to do this, so you might ask: 'What does loving my neighbour look like on social media?' If I post a comment, does it build somebody up or knock them down? If I like or share something, is that going to love them as I would like to be loved?

Thirdly, God's love is a safe refuge for us when the world becomes a hard place. We all know that social media can expose us to cruel comments and comparison. It's not always a great place to be, but we can share with our kids that God's love is where you can be reminded about how you're a beloved and valued child of the king. It's also a place where we can find strength to face our emotions, fears and insecurities.

To help with that, you could chat about bits of the Bible which show how to find refuge in God when the world seems against us. Elijah retreated into depression after his mighty conquering of the prophets of Baal but met God in the quietness. There's Mordecai and the Jewish nation, Jeremiah complaining after being put in the stocks, and even Jesus at his trial and crucifixion. Look at those stories and ask what helped when everything was against them. Share your own stories of humiliation, so your children see that this is a necessary but nasty side of life, one we can get through with God's help. Session 7 of our free Parenting for Faith course, 'Prayer ministry with children', will help us help our kids connect with God when it's tough.

Follow-up

- 'Gaming' (p. 101) and 'Pornography' (p. 138) chapters
- parentingforfaith.org/post/equipping-kids-to-live-well-with-social-media
- Katharine Hill, *Left to Their Own Devices? Confident parenting in a world of screens* (Kilfinan Press, 2024)
- parentingforfaith.org/course/7-prayer-ministry-for-children
- parentingforfaith.org/topics/tv-film-and-social-media

Next steps

- If your child isn't on social media, what will help you judge if and when they are ready for it? How could you help them take their first steps?
- What's been your own experience – good and bad – of social media? How could you create windows into and frame how God has helped you in decisions around and experiences of social media?
- What might your child or teen need to know about how to engage with social media in a way that is good for them and good for others?

S

SPORT

Competitiveness

The world is super competitive. Our children are going to land in hypercompetitive environments, so they need to learn how to model Jesus in that. We need to give kids permission to be competitive. There's certainly nothing wrong with winning.

Christian parents often say to me: 'My kid's so competitive – how do I help them just enjoy it?' I point out that, for their child, being competitive *is* how they're enjoying it. The question is how to be a disciple of Jesus while being hyper-competitive, because we don't want to switch that competitiveness off – that's their God-given character. It's how they do that in light of who Jesus is. In my household, I use sport as a vehicle to try to coach my kids into good discipleship habits.

Sport and discipleship

Discipleship is about practice, and sport is one of the naturally easy ways to try something, test it out, step outside your comfort zone and reflect. Even a child who doesn't enjoy sport will have PE lessons, so that gives you an opportunity to help them think through the little steps they can take.

Is that not what discipleship is? Little steps we take to find our place in God's world or to help ourselves become more like Jesus? The conversation about sport won't always come back to Jesus, but when my child is facing obstacles or difficult relationships, how am I helping coach kindness, honesty and good boundaries, so they develop as a human being? And how am I coaching them so they use their support network around them?

Sport is a fantastic vehicle for things which are fundamental to discipleship: community, practice, making mistakes, reflecting, reviewing, and learning how Jesus informs our decision-making.

Weekly sport is a great opportunity to practise being gracious in victory and defeat, getting on with a team-mate you don't like, and encouraging others. You don't have to turn those into mini-sermons – they could be games: 'I wonder how many encouragements you can give to… today?'

Creating windows through sport

Social media obviously has its challenges, but it also gives us an insight into people's lives. It's a great place to help our kids look at their heroes' whole life:

- 'They're struggling with injury – I wonder what they're thinking about that?'
- 'They've had a really good result – what might your good result be, this season?'
- 'They pray before a game – what might be a good rhythm for you before a game?'

Social media gives you someone to follow *with* your child, a conversation prompt to help them start to think about some of the bigger global issues around the type of human they want to be in light of their Christian faith.

The challenges are that Christians express their faith in different ways, and also most professional sportspeople's social media is curated by a team. This can help your kid develop a little bit of discernment around following people on social media.

Framing sport with God in the centre

This ultimately comes down to what we model as parents, and how we structure the week. I would want to have compassion on a kid who gets excited about something, because that's just the thing that's pushing their buttons at the moment, but to do it in a worshipful way so it's not competing with, but an extension of, their discipleship.

I want to be:

- giving thanks for the hobby and opportunities
- praising them for the Jesus-like qualities they show in sport
- praying with them beforehand
- teaching my kids the habit of prayer before any activity

Then I want to make sure we have regular times when sport isn't part of what we're doing, when we are just family together. I'd want to teach them how to worship through that, rather than make it an idol.

This isn't a weekly pep talk from a parent. I'll say to my kids, 'I love to watch you play and I think Jesus has really gifted you like this.' We are making it clear that, for us, Jesus is in the centre of this sports narrative. I share good stories of sportspeople who have had to stop because of injury, age or being dropped, so our kids realise that sport is not a forever story.

Sunday sports

Every sporting family has to resolve this issue. It's a great conversation about priorities as a family: how you juggle using your God-given gifts and your desire to be part of a worshipping community. I don't think that's a problem at all, because kids are going to have to wrestle with similar things throughout their life. How do they juggle the tension of non-Christian friends and the diary factors that come along with that?

Lots of middle-class Christian parents have an addiction to their children being in clubs (disclaimer: us too!), so this prompts conversation, reflection and opportunities to make decisions based around your family values.

High-level sports

If your child is competing at a high level, celebrate it! But help them be grounded. Get your church praying for them and showing lots of interest in them, especially if their attendance is difficult because they're excelling at sport.

Finally, get the church to celebrate them when they're attending services, rather than bemoan when they're not, so that the kids know they have a home, a deep harbour in church that will welcome them back when sport isn't giving all that they need it to.

Follow-up

- non-perfectdad.co.uk (Richard Shorter)
- Richard also appeared on S4E6: Success and failure in sport

Next steps

- What one or two things stood out for you from this chapter?
- If your kid is involved in Sunday sport, how could they stay part of their church community and engage with what you value about church?
- What might your child learn about God or faith from sport? How could you help with that?

S

SUPERNATURAL

RACHEL TURNER S1E86

In both Old and New Testaments, supernatural stuff is happening; for example: the witch from Endor who spoke to dead people (1 Samuel 28); visions with dry bones coming to life (Ezekiel 37); demon possession (Mark 5 and others); idol worship, mediums and omens. In the modern world we're exposed to fantasy worlds of zombies and monsters – so how do we walk with our kids through this?

Firstly, we're commanded in scripture: 'Don't be afraid.' When I look over scripture, I see the boldness of the people of God. They weren't afraid, they walked right into it, dealt with it and moved on. Helping our kids find boldness in the face of the supernatural and paranormal is the beginning of our journey.

Some kids will have questions like, 'What is a witch?' or 'Are there ghosts in the Bible?' Some kids may need it framed historically: people have always tried to find power that isn't theirs, because they wanted to be more powerful. So that's why you find witches or mediums who try to contact the dead; they're searching for power beyond them. Or your child may simply need framing that there's God stuff and not-God stuff. Anything not of God isn't something we need to be afraid of, because God is more powerful.

Whether demons or ghosts, God is so much more powerful than anything. He carries all authority over everything, natural and supernatural. This isn't good and evil in a tussle. God would completely crush anything evil in the world at a thought, and he gives us authority to do that too. Whatever's out there, we can connect with God and hold strong in the face of it.

Not everything is supernatural: sometimes our brains just make up stuff. When I was three, I remember believing that sharks were coming up the drain to eat my feet. Even now, occasionally, I'll be in the shower and get this wave of fear that a shark is coming, before realising it's not real. Sometimes our brains do weird things, but we can find our peace and grab on to God. Sometimes this is about framing what makes us scared and why, so we can understand the world around us.

We can ask curious questions too. If your kid is convinced there's a ghost in their room, ask: 'Where did that idea come from? Is that something you've seen in the Bible? What makes you scared about that?' Often we feel scared because we don't understand, so fear becomes mysterious, or we misunderstand and think it's more powerful than it is. So it can be useful to go on this journey of learning not to be scared. Wherever you are on the theological spectrum, helping your kid find their peace amid fear is helpful, so they can see where God is in it and know how to engage with it.

We also see in scripture a command not to mess with it. Our kids need to have healthy boundaries around things like Ouija boards or other weird games, to ask, 'Is this delighting in God or is this trying to mess with something that isn't of God?' They can tell themselves, 'I'm not supposed to be scared of it, but I'm also not going to mess with it.' There's a lot you can do to face things that aren't of God, and when you make kids feel powerful, that's when the fear goes away and they're ready to say no.

We can teach our kids how to respond and find peace when something's going on that is not of God. We can show them how to say: 'No – nothing gets to come in this room that is not of God. Fear, go away in the name of Jesus.' Then give them ways to find their God-centre again, whether it's particular music they play, a list of truths or a Bible verse. That empowerment is powerful.

Follow-up

- 'Halloween' (p. 106) chapter
- **parentingforfaith.org/post/summary-talking-about-the-supernatural**

Next steps

- Is your child aware of the supernatural? What do you think their understanding or experience is?
- What might help your child understand that God is more powerful than anything evil, so they don't need to be afraid? How could you coach them in what to do if they come across anything supernatural that disturbs or scares them?

U

UNIVERSITY

PIPPA ELMES
(SUMMER EDIT 1, BETWEEN SEASONS 6 AND 7)

Spiritual landscape

Going to university has always been a pivotal moment for young adults – a time of stepping into independence and new opportunities. But how students are engaging with spirituality looks different now. A huge number don't have any knowledge at all about Jesus. That presents some challenges, but also means that the good news about Jesus is genuinely 'news'. In a recent survey we ran, about 76% said they'd go to church if invited by a friend.

Opportunities for our children's faith journey at university

University is a great opportunity for our young people to choose church for themselves, many for the first time. Make them aware of the range of choice: 'Did you know about this? Is this something you'd like my help with or would you like to do it yourself?' Fusion's **studentlinkup.org** helps students connect to churches. You know your kids best – will they want help? Will you sit down and do this together? Or are they independent, so that you could say something like: 'Here's a resource that helps you choose a church. You get to choose it, I'm not going to choose it for you.'

University was one of the first times I developed ecumenical friendships with people passionate about Jesus but who disagreed with me on certain theological topics. It makes you ask: 'Why do I believe this, and where is that rooted? Is it rooted in scripture or in my family?'

University also comes with a level of vulnerability, which is why connecting with a church is important. We can forget that as young people go off, they're engaging in an environment where they're not known. Many students have told me that they walked into church and didn't feel welcome. Some of that is a lesson for us as the church, but some of it is because many students' prior church experience was being part of the same church community for 18 years. You're known deeply in that place, and now you're needing to start from scratch with new relationships.

Much of what the church takes for granted in terms of hospitality feels exceptional to non-Christian students. I remember inviting a new student and her housemates for lunch. They couldn't believe she was going for lunch at someone's house at the end of her second week at university. The welcome of students is something the whole church family can take part in. So much of the church's gift is the multigenerational element that students are often really hungry for.

University can help our school leavers grow in communication of their faith. How do I communicate my understanding of who God is with grace, love and clarity among other Christians, but also among people who don't know Jesus? Sharing faith and seeing others come to know Jesus is fantastic for our faith. One of the blessings of having students within your church community is that they're often passionate about sharing their faith. Seeing students come to church, meet Jesus, be baptised and join the fellowship is an inspiration to all of us to ask, 'Are we doing that?'

Tips for parents

You can start the conversation by framing: 'I'm so proud of you, not because of what you've achieved but because of who you are. You're going to be a real gift to where you're going, and I'm excited for what God has for you.' This is the start of a new relationship, as they step into adulthood. You'll learn new ways of talking together and being together and your relationship will shift – so share your excitement, that you want to come alongside them. Be open that there will be ups and downs, but you're going to be their biggest cheerleader all the way. Whether or not you feel like you have loads of wisdom to give, the important thing is the relationship, speaking the affirmation that you're here with them.

We can frame that how God has made them is fantastic, and the best thing they can do is bring their true, authentic self – including their faith – to new relationships early on. In the first term, everyone's trying to make the best impression, and that can only last so long. Encourage them to develop friend-ships with people they feel safe with, who they can trust and with whom they can be themselves.

Pray for your young people. I don't say that flippantly. I've spoken to students who've returned to faith at university, telling me of a grandparent, parent or friend who had been praying for them for years. Faithful prayer is powerful. Calling on the Holy Spirit to be present in our children's lives is significant. I'm already aware with my two-year-old that I'm just not in control of her faith journey. As much as I can pray, model and partner with her in helping her discover Jesus, at the end of the day I'm relying on the Holy Spirit for that journey within her. That's the same at university.

Who does your young person trust? We raise young people in community, and there'll be others in their life who have influence: grandparents, family friends, godparents, youth workers. Can you involve them? They might be someone your child will call when struggling.

We can encourage a spirit of adventure in our young people. For most young people, their world will have been geographically and socially small, but now they're going to meet students from everywhere. There's this amaz-ing richness of culture, and faith comes into that too. There will be more to learn from people of different theologies and cultures. So much of what I've learned about God has come from friends who aren't British, who have a cultural spiritual heritage in Jesus. They often know how to do community in powerful ways, and they worship and pray in ways I could only long to have the perseverance for.

Tips for sending churches

This is a significant milestone on our young people's journey, and we want to mark it with them. There may also be people who are going into the workplace or an apprenticeship. You might want to get them up at the front of church, sharing where they're going and praying for them. Some churches create prayer cards for individuals, with their name, where they're going to university/work, what they're studying and what they're excited and nervous about. People in church can opt to 'adopt' a student to pray for.

Getting together with others going to university is something you can encourage or facilitate. Why not meet up, have dinner, chat and celebrate together? Think about who else you might draw into it. Are there other local churches who have one or two students?

Celebrate your students when they come back. Christmas holidays are important as a debrief. How's it been? Let's celebrate what God's been doing, but also acknowledge it may have been challenging. Have you found a church yet? So often there'll be an influx of students in church in January because parents, carers and youth workers have reminded their young people over Christmas to get stuck in.

Follow-up

- parentingforfaith.org/topics/transitions
- fusionmovement.org
- studentlinkup.org

Next steps

- If you are the parent or carer of a student, what conversations do you want to have with them about faith, church and university?
- If you have a teen, how can you begin to prepare them for the time they leave home and have to choose a church?
- If you have school leavers or students in your church, how can you come alongside and encourage them?

WALKING AWAY FROM FAITH

SARAH WALTON AND LINDA GREEN S7E9

When your child is walking away

SARAH

If your child is walking away from faith, you are not alone.

When I walked away from faith when I was young, the thing that stood out to me was that my mum and my dad didn't give up on me. I was retreating from the people who loved me the most and could have helped me the most. I hadn't grasped the grace of the gospel and felt I wasn't acceptable, so it felt easier to run from it than towards it.

When you look at the story of the prodigal son, one of the things we glean from it is the patience of the father. He was always waiting and ready to receive his son when he came back. He wasn't angry and resentful of his son; he was patiently waiting for him. As parents, how do we do that? We keep asking questions, keep trying to pursue them, keep trying to understand what's happening in their life that we're not seeing, or what's under the surface of the anger that's just the outer working of the pain they may be facing.

The very strong will that resistant kids tend to have is also the strong will that God can use and do mighty things through. We can help our kids see that they have a strong, determined will and that this is something God can use amazingly. This is not a negative thing to get rid of, it just needs to be redirected. Our kids may not want to hear that right now, but we can pray that way.

Love speaks more than we realise. You can continue to say, 'I don't agree with what you're doing, but I love you and I'm here for you, ready to receive you, praying for you and fighting for you.' Your child's behaviour may not show gratitude for that type of parenting, but I believe that God can bring that out when he reaches their heart.

Lastly, hold on to hope. No matter how old our child may be – we may have a 40-year-old child who is still resisting the faith, and the fact that they do grieves us – but as long as we're alive and they're alive, there is still hope.

Standing firm

LINDA

When my daughter Sarah was rejecting Jesus, the question I had to ask myself was: what does it mean to worship God above all else, when you are so desperately trying to love your children and husband well, and you want them to love you?

I was tested in this when Sarah asked me why I couldn't be like her friends' mums – which usually meant letting her do what she wanted, more than what we believed was best for her. When you're striving to be a faithful parent, but your child sees you as the enemy, it can be tempting to cave in. God helped me understand that what my daughter most needed was for me to love her unconditionally with both Christ's love and truth, offering a window of gospel grace to her in every way possible. Grace meant learning to be like Jesus to a daughter who didn't even want to talk about him. I quickly learned I couldn't do that without relying on his grace myself. Some of the ways this worked itself out were: learning not to respond when she said something hurtful; giving her a hug and saying I love you when I was hurting inside; letting her know that our love for her wasn't based on her behaviour and that we would never stop fighting for her; reminding her how much God loved her. We show them his love when we demonstrate unconditional love, even when we're disagreeing with their choices.

I learned to ask forgiveness of Sarah for times I had judged her, humbling myself, providing another window that could point her to the gospel.

Encouragement

LINDA

It's important to remember that we are all prodigals in God's eyes. Apart from his mercy, we are all rebels who deserve his judgement. That humbles us and keeps us looking to the Lord for what he can do. When your child's words and behaviour tempt you to believe that you have failed as a parent, remember that God's grace is made perfect in weakness. He promises to equip us to parent our wandering children as we turn to him for wisdom and strength.

Then, when the enemy comes at you with a feeling of shame, accusing you that it's your fault that your child isn't following the Lord, we are to rest in God's all-sufficient grace. The truth is we can do everything right and our children can still walk away from him.

Finally, when you don't see immediate answers to your prayers, keep praying. Remember God's timing is very often different from ours, and he works in ways that we might not expect or could even imagine. He simply asks us to trust his unfailing love and his faithfulness. And he really is a faithful God.

Follow-up

- 'Church – helping kids engage with it' (p. 44), 'Church hurt' (p. 49) and 'Doubt' (p. 70) chapters
- Sarah Walton and Linda Green, *He Gives More Grace: 30 reflections for the ups and downs of motherhood through the years* (The Good Book Company, 2023)

Next steps

- If you have a child who has walked away from faith, reread the story of the prodigal son (Luke 15), asking God to open your heart to what he is showing you.
- What can help you 'stand firm' on what you believe is right?
- Consider your own faith journey. Where did you waver? What happened? What was God doing?

W

WORSHIP

SIMON PARRY AND BECKY SEDGWICK

Kids and worship

SIMON S1E84

There's great strength in having songs written for children in worship. There are some great grown-up songs to use in kids' worship too, but the key thing about kids' worship is having songs they can relate to, they can engage with and that they lyrically understand. For example, the classic kids' song 'Father God I wonder' has a simplicity about it that kids get. They can sing it, understand it and remember the lyrics.

As a family, we have worship music playing constantly in the house and car. Our kids have devices now, so we'll walk round the house and each bedroom has a different song blasting out and each kid is singing it. We listen to pop music too, but we've modelled that worship is part of our life. It's not just Sunday; it's wherever we are as a family. There are times when I don't want to listen to worship music, I'd like to listen to something to take my mind off church, but this is important. We model it as the norm, and that's been super powerful. I love the fact that our kids' playlists are a real mix. As parents, that's been something we've pushed as being part of our life as much as listening to Radio 2.

You want kids to own the songs. Just like we have favourite worship songs that we'd naturally turn to in particular seasons, I want that for kids. I want them to have songs they love jumping around to, but also songs they can relate to and cling on to in times of need.

Encouraging songwriting

SIMON S1E72

I was leading a kids' group at New Wine, and we had a sense that God was going to give the kids some new worship songs – bearing in mind these are five-to-seven-year-olds. It felt crazy, but also right, so we prayed and told the kids. There was a real excitement and we had dribs and drabs of songs about bunny rabbits, the sun and moon, all kinds of stuff. I was like, 'Oh my word, Lord, is this it?!'

Then on the Wednesday, a little boy called Sam handed me a scrap of paper he'd written on. As soon as I held it, I just felt God say, 'This is it.' The song was called 'God is great': 'God is great, my God is great, he's brilliant, he's made me brave, he's given me strength, I love to say my God is great.' We put some music to his words, then taught the song in the main big top all-age family celebration. The place went wild! It was awesome to see God had given a young boy a simple song of praise that thousands worshipped to. The following year we recorded it; it was sung all over the world in different languages.

We don't need an amazing, finished masterpiece to be able to worship God. Over the years we've done songwriting workshops with kids and sung their songs in Sunday school and church. Some of them have been cheesy – but even if we never sing it again, the encouragement it's given the child, or the fact that God speaks to an adult through that lyric, is worth it. I would encourage any kid who wants to write songs to do it.

Some songs will never see the light of day. I remember a story about John Wimber – he wrote new songs every day, but some of them were just for him and God; no one else ever heard them. I love that. If a kid wants to write new songs every day, go for it, and if no one else hears them, that doesn't matter because all this is for the audience of one. Even if it drives you nuts, if the song is the cheesiest thing ever, encourage them to keep going, because you never know what fruit might come of it.

The power of songs

Songs are much easier for us to remember than just words. Many years ago, in a bad bit of my life, I had an experience where a song I'd learnt as a tiny child was used by God to speak to me powerfully and profoundly about my situation.

I once heard about some early missionaries to China. Travelling from village to village, they would teach a set of twelve songs which gave the whole gospel. Then they'd move on to another area, translate them into the next language and so on. The reasoning was that it would help people remember God's truth when they didn't have access to a Bible in their own language.

When I became a children's worker, I realised the importance of picking songs which would contain truths these kids could retain 20–30 years down the line. We decided to do an experiment: for six months we sang just twelve songs containing important truths which we hoped as a result would be embedded into these kids' brains.

If you're listening to songs with your kids at home, there are so many out there, so here are the criteria we used for picking ours, just in case you think it might be interesting to try at home:

1 **Songs that give a broad and balanced view of God.** Not just intimate songs of God loving me and me loving God, but songs that contain a broad view of who God is and what he does.

2 **Songs that contain the truth about the whole story of God.** As far as possible, songs that will help children understand different bits of the big story of salvation.

3 **Songs in different styles of worship.** Songs which expose the children to different types of worship, so they can discover what helps them connect with God best.

The songs you choose to listen to as a family can be phenomenally powerful in conveying God's truth.

Follow-up

- parentingforfaith.org/post/summary-worship
- youtube.com/fWJCQ8sLi3o (to listen to 'God is Great')

Next steps

- What worship songs do your children listen to and love?
- What do you think about the idea of deliberately picking a limited number of songs so your kids can learn truth from them?
- How could you encourage your children to have a go at writing their own worship songs, if that's something that interests them?

APPENDIX I
THE PARENTING
FOR FAITH
KEY TOOLS AND VALUES

Our vision and approach

At Parenting for Faith, our vision is to see families equipped to confidently parent their children and teens into a vibrant, two-way relationship with God.

We believe that God's plan for children's and teens' discipleship is rooted in Deuteronomy 6:4–9:

> Hear, O Israel: the Lord our God, the Lord is one. Love the Lord your God with all your heart and with all your soul and with all your strength. These commandments that I give you today are to be on your hearts. Impress them on your children. Talk about them when you sit at home and when you walk along the road, when you lie down and when you get up. Tie them as symbols on your hands and bind them on your foreheads. Write them on the door-frames of your houses and on your gates.

Discipleship takes place in the ordinary everyday, whatever that looks like for a family. God has positioned parents and carers to show their children the reality of a day-to-day life with God. Faith is discovered and explored in the same way any other passion or skill is – by seeing, copying, talking, questioning and growing in understanding – and this takes place best in the family which knows and loves their children the best and has the most time with them.

Because every child, every teen and every family is unique, we don't suggest a one-size-fits-all approach. There is no one right way to help kids meet and know God. So we help people find their next step on this journey of parenting for faith. Many of the extracts from the podcast in this book are examples of how different parents, carers and families are working out what real, everyday discipleship is like for them.

God's design has always been that parents and carers don't disciple in isolation. He has placed them in a wider community of extended family, friends and church communities, all of whom have their part to play in children and young people's journey of meeting and knowing God. So we've also included extracts from podcasts with people who have spent time thinking about how children and young people grow in their relationship with God and have shared their ideas and experiences with us.

Our Key Tools

In many chapters you'll find references to the five Key Tools, which are at the heart of the Parenting for Faith approach.

They will equip you to proactively help your family or the children and young people in your life meet and know God. And if you are a church leader or if you work with children and young people in church, you'll find they work for you too.

These five Key Tools are, in many ways, similar to the ordinary parenting skills you already have: we've simply shown how they work for discipleship too.

Tool #1: Creating windows

This tool builds on the way God has designed our brains to learn best – by watching and trying things for ourselves. Creating windows is a way to allow kids to glimpse what your relationship with God looks like, so they can learn how to have a real two-way connection with him themselves.

Tool #2: Framing

Framing is all about explaining – what God is doing, why things happen, who he is. Framing shows kids how God works in all of life, helps them explore the Bible and relate it to everyday life and work through any question they might have.

Tool #3: Unwinding

This is an important tool for helping kids to grow a balanced and healthy view of God. It can be easy to slip into a lopsided view, and this tool helps to gently unwind misconceptions, building in a broad and balanced understanding of who God is.

Tool #4: Chat and catch

This tool encourages children in prayer and hearing God's voice – chatting to him about everything that is on their hearts and catching his response, however he chooses to speak. Chat and catch helps children and teens to connect directly with God at any time, in all circumstances, wherever they are, without needing their parent or carer to be the 'high priest' interceding on their behalf.

Tool #5: Surfing the waves

This tool helps us spot what God is doing in a child or young person's life. All kids are different, and God's purposes for them are different. Learn to identify their 'waves' and support them as interests and passions come and go.

For more about the five Key Tools see **parentingforfaith.org/tools.**

We're here for you at every age and stage

Children grow and change. Families grow and change. We all grow and change. We want to resource you for every step of the journey, whether your children are newborns or adults themselves, whatever challenges they may be facing. We also know that being a parent or carer and a church leader brings particular challenges, and that grandparents longing to see their grandchildren meet and know God need resourcing too.

Do continue to listen to our podcast to hear what Parenting for Faith looks like in all sorts of situations and all sorts of lives.

We also have books and courses for every stage and a website packed full of stories and wisdom for everyone.

Our courses

- Parenting for Faith
- Parenting Teens for a Life of Faith
- Babies and Toddlers
- Parenting as a Church Leader
- Grandparenting for Faith

For more about our courses see **parentingforfaith.org/courses**

Our books

- *Grandparenting for Faith: Sharing God with the children you love the most* by Becky Sedgwick (2024)
- *Being God's Child: A parent's guide* by Anna Hawken (2023)
- *Parenting Teens for a Life of Faith: Helping teens meet and know God* by Rachel Turner (2022)
- *Comfort in Uncertain Times: Helping children draw close to God through biblical stories of anxiety, loss and transition* by Rachel Turner (2022)
- *Babies and Toddlers: Nurturing your child's spiritual life* by Rachel Turner (2021)
- *Parenting as a Church Leader: Helping your family thrive* by Rachel Turner (2020)
- *Parenting Children for a Life of Faith: Helping children meet and know God* (omnibus edition) by Rachel Turner (2018)
- *It Takes a Church to Raise a Parent: Creating a culture where parenting for faith can flourish* by Rachel Turner (2018)
- *Comfort in the Darkness: Helping children draw close to God through biblical stories of night-time and sleep* by Rachel Turner (2016)

We have lots of Parenting for Faith titles, which you can find here: **parentingforfaith.org/topics/shop**.

We regularly update our website and other courses, so do subscribe to receive up-to-date information – **parentingforfaith.org/keep-touch**.

APPENDIX II
INDEX OF
CONTRIBUTORS

BRF Ministries

Inspiring people of all ages to grow in Christian faith

BRF Ministries is the home of Anna Chaplaincy, BRF Resources, Messy Church and Parenting for Faith

As a charity, our work would not be possible without fundraising and gifts in wills.
To find out more and to donate,
visit brf.org.uk/give or call +44 (0)1235 462305

Registered with
FUNDRAISING
REGULATOR